Time and the Human Condition

An Exploration on Perspective

Partap Singh

Alight Publications 2005

Time and the Human Condition
By Partap Singh

First Edition Published in January, 2005

Alight Publications
PO Box 930
Union City, CA 94587

http://www.Alightbooks.com

Time and the Human Condition © 2005. All rights reserved by Partap Singh and Alight Publications. No part of this publication may be reproduced, stored in a retrieval system or database, or transmitted in any form or by any means electronic, mechanical, photocopying, recording, or otherwise without the prior written approval of the author or publisher.

ISBN 1-931833-12-5

Printed in the United States of America

Time and the Human Condition

Contents

Introduction / 1

Part 1: On The Nature Of Time
Time in Classical Physics and its Relationship To Light / 10
Perspective and Quantum Machines / 26
The Ability to Contemplate Eternity is not a Survival Trait / 33

Part 2: Purpose in Life
Basic Possibilities After This Life / 40
The Purpose of This Life in Light of Eternity / 50
Cultivating the Human Garden – Legitimate Communities / 66

Part 3: Perspective
On Possibilities / 83
Time and Perspective / 86
Perspective on the Past: Oral versus written Tradition / 96
Perspective on the Past: The Attraction of the New and the Polarization of the Old / 104
Perspective on the Past: Why have the Illusion of money, but not Of Peace? / 111

Part 4: Applying Perspective
Key Aspects / 119
On Education / 123
On Government and Party Politics / 131
On Law, Justice and Order / 141
On Reality, Fantasy, and Vicarious Experience / 148

Part 5: Human Understanding
Sensation and Reflection /154
Time and Stress / 162
On the Nature of Philosophy / 173
Time and Love / 180

Conclusion: Means Without Ends / 195

Appendix I / 207

Appendix II / 211

Time and the Human Condition

Introduction

"Time is the fire in which we burn"
Delmore Schwartz

When people recall the past, it comes back to them only a little more vividly than their dreams do. We have trouble remembering more than isolated images, and sometimes it seems incomprehensible to us that we did certain things, or said certain things. It is all a haze, and might as well have been imagined. Even if we had sharper memories, and a few people do have the ability to recall minute details in their own past, that memory would be limited by the short spans of our lives. To provide any perspective on the past, we have to rely on histories and traditions passed down to us that may have long lost their meaning.

When people think of the Greeks, Romans, or any ancient civilization, they see caricatures, images that seem outside of reality, not people they can relate to and learn from. How can they derive useful meaning from peoples that seem so alien? Also, historians are themselves focused on the modern moment – they are looking at the past only to explain something in the present, and can therefore miss the key issues and ideas in their studies. History is therefore inadequate for giving a clear perspective on the past. As for cultural traditions, they are constantly being reinvented in subtle ways because people forget why certain actions were necessary, and assign meanings to other actions that were not significant before. So, in all cases, the way we look at the past tells us more about the

Introduction

present. The actual past remains a vague imagination, with images and artifacts but no substance.

The future is clearly a dream to us. We shape the future with our present thoughts, and our immediate actions. But the same can be true of the past – historians are not the only ones whose present experiences determine what values they see coming out of the past. That is true for all of us. We forget those things that are no longer meaningful, and those forgotten things can often be completely lost. That which is lost is inaccessible to generations in the future, so that the loss shapes their lives in turn. Because the affects are often subtle, the only times we can actually see this occurring is in the midst of major social-political change. The greatest such change in recorded history is probably the fall of the Roman Empire, in which much of Greco-Roman learning was lost. The Greeks had known quite clearly that the world was a globe and had measured its circumference to within a thousand miles of the actual distance, but this information was lost for over a thousand years, resulting in a number of miscalculations by Columbus. The reason for the loss was simple – with the spread of Christianity, the knowledge of non-Christians, with the exception of Aristotle, was dismissed. Many classics that have survived to this day were kept in limited access church libraries, and in some cases used as scratch paper. The Greco-Roman past gave way to a Christian present, and the present shaped the past by forcibly forgetting it.

Ultimately, the aggregate of all our expectations can come as close to revealing the future as the sum of our memories can reveal the past. And, in fact, if such a summation could be taken, it would be extremely revealing, though still limited. The key is that the future is different from the past in one way – we can have an impact on it. We have simply studied the past more, and written our thoughts about it coherently, so there is the illusion of a difference. If we wrote as much about the future, we would quickly realize the illusion. No subject of study explores the future in the way history explores the past. Practically the only times people try to predict the future is when gambling, fortune-telling, in science-fiction novels, and when polling to see who might win a political race. The future should be taken more seriously. Even creating a subject of study, like history with all its limitations, would be an improvement. The subject would simply be the study of possibilities, perhaps bringing the abstraction of statistics to practical use. This would be especially useful in democracies, since voters could have the whole range of possibilities laid out before them, with detailed analysis and competing opinions, which would ideally avoid the oversimplified dualities presented to the public today. The only application of statistics in practical use is through polls, which only present the two or three possibilities that people are already aware of.

After looking at the past and the future, one might ask how present reality should be understood. In respect to time, it is the infinitesimal moment between the past and the future. It is the moment between the two dreams where we might actually have an effect on things, to move things in a certain direction. This definition should show how ridiculous it is for people to demand realism, or to dismiss certain solutions as mere idealism – in this case the political meaning of idealism, referring to a devotion to ideas over the current situation, which is contrasted with political realism, also known as "realpolitik", which emphasizes the practical situation over theory or ideals. Political realists have been dominant since the days of Machiavelli – one of the founders of "realpolitik" at the end of the 15th century, and idealistic beliefs have been dismissed or submerged ever since. An example of this is the wanton transgressions against the Universal Declaration of Human Rights, which is an idealistic document.

Introduction

But idealism is infinite while realism is miniscule. Realism demands that neither the past nor the future should be taken into account, which is an incredibly shortsighted approach that is in part due to a pessimistic view of human nature. The basic reasoning behind realism is that if idealism drove change, it would inevitably go too far, leading to ruin. However, the whole point of the miniscule moment between the past and the future is to strive to reach the ideal. If everyone in the world, at this moment, decided that there could be peace in the world, and that they themselves would not disrupt it, then there would be world peace. If you think that such an idea is an illusion, consider money for a moment. Money only has value because we agree that it has value at every moment we use it and accept it as payment. It is a collective illusion we have established that allows our society to function. Which begs the question, why do we have the illusion of money, but not one of world peace?

We get caught in this moment of reality, and people refuse to escape it lest they lose their own grounding. The fear is that, since the dream is infinite, there will not be anything to hang onto. Now is definite. Reality is a perch, the smaller the better because it becomes easier to understand. On this perch, people can forget the past and ignore the future. The perch is necessary, of course, because the state of our consciousness limits our perception of the past and the future. The problem occurs when people neglect to reach into the past and future. There has to be a balance between focusing on the moment, and pondering the stretches of time, as long as our consciousness prevents us from managing both simultaneously. Unfortunately, in the modern day of high-speed communication and high stress life, it is increasingly difficult to avoid getting trapped by the moment.

The past is frightening because we cannot change it, yet it affects us. The future is frightening because we do not know what is coming, and the unknown tends to spark fear before anything else. If the future inspired more curiosity, perhaps we would be willing to study it in greater detail. Reality keeps us busy – it is full of things to do. Forget being curious – there's television! Now you can experience everything vicariously, letting others take the risk and dream the dreams. The so-called "reality" television shows let the viewers stay stuck in their moment of reality watching men and women being miserable facing innumerable ordeals as they dream – of all stupid things to dream for – of winning an impressive sum of money.

These are not exactly revelations, and I am sure others before me have considered all of these things. However, as with much of what follows, I feel it needs to be said because I have not read it. This is a book about perspective – most directly perspective through and about time. In everything, I hope to encourage the reader to avoid simple dualities, and look through a range of possibilities and viewpoints. By looking at time itself, we will see that there is a great deal to gain, not only in the realm of perspectives but also in raw quality of thought, from examining and synthesizing a range of ideas.

The key to the human condition is the fact that our lives, compared to what they could be, are fairly short. Nothing is more important in determining how we deal with the future and what we imagine to be reality, than this simple fact. Having to cope with this problem from the earliest of days, people have contemplated the existence of an afterlife. In most cases, the afterlife is a plane of existence outside our current one, and is also the realm of the deity or deities that might have created the universe, so that purposes like "to be one with God" are most clearly meant to be fulfilled in the afterlife. Most of the discussions that follow will assume that there is an afterlife, but it is not necessary for the reader to agree with

Introduction

that point of view to appreciate the discussions on time and perceptions. The sections on cultural phenomena, education, government, and law, all show how perspective is necessary and can be applied to constructive change in this life.

In any case, there are many possibilities for what the afterlife might be like, but let us first consider the "good" afterlife, or something resembling the Christian heaven, and what has been said about it so far. It is reputedly eternal – a key and very enticing component, naturally, since the desire to escape time and transcend the bounds of our short lives is so strong. Even if such a heaven is a fairly placid, static place, simply knowing that there is somewhere to go after this life comes as a relief. According to some accounts, heaven is far more real than this world, and this life is only an illusion, a dream, which seems fair enough. In Christianity and many other belief systems, the afterlife is portrayed as a plane of existence with a radically different sense of time than we experience on Earth. There are Hindu stories of Krishna, for instance, which suggest that half an hour for the god is equivalent to twelve years on Earth. The persistent trouble with the six days of creation in Genesis is another indication of a more interesting sense of time among the divine, and since the plane of the divine is that of the afterlife, we can assume that a more metaphoric version of the flow of time exists in the Christian heaven.

There will be further discussion of the various possible afterlives and their implications in a later section. For now, I will propose that all time in any permanent afterlife – in other words, one that does not require a return to this realm of existence – would be as tangible as the moment-by-moment reality we live in. All of eternity would be "now", with no difference between the past and the future – all of it being equally accessible. This would certainly be a higher plane of understanding. Many of the problems of our current existence would be solved, as there would no longer be fear of the past or future, since those words would no longer have any meaning. The basis of this assumption, and how time might be perceived differently will be explained further in the sections on physics and our ability to contemplate eternity.

Since reality is the time in which we can affect change, people in an afterlife with this higher consciousness of time would be able to affect change for all of eternity. Eternity, in fact, has a much more interesting meaning if taken alongside this assumption about the afterlife, since it would be both all time and an instant. It also means an end to the fears of this life, and the ultimate in perspective. Perspective is the key, and will be discussed frequently, since it is so intimately tied to time and alleviating the irrational fears of this life. The discussions will deal with subjects like culture's interactions with time and the ways traditions are passed down from generation to generation.

An afterlife that consists of an eternal 'now' begs the question of how we get from our current conception of time to that one, how we get from the earthly consciousness to a more heavenly one. It is certainly possible to assume the most obvious solution – that death is the transition to the alternate plane of existence, and therefore provides all that will be required for the afterlife. On the other hand, it is also possible to take a more religious view – perhaps God can determine whether a person, based on his or her actions in life, deserves the heavenly consciousness, or does not deserve it and therefore should retain the moment-by-moment perception of time, for the rest of time, while boiling in a fiery pit. More convincing, however, is the idea that we somehow need to expand our consciousness, transcend the limitations we currently face, and thereby in this life, or perhaps after reincarnating through a few lives, prepare ourselves for the higher plane of existence. In any case, all these and other

Introduction

possibilities will be discussed further, and they are already familiar to us except in the way they relate to the time aspect of the afterlife.

Of course, the very idea that the afterlife is eternal has been essential to its popularity. But considering how time affects us, and gaining a greater perspective on it, will serve us regardless of whether there is an afterlife or not. Through the more cultural discussions it will be clear that many social struggles are affected by distorted senses of time and lack of perspective. Ultimately, time is the key to the human condition, and the single most important reason why we believe in a life after this one.

Part 1
On The Nature Of Time

On the Nature of Time

Time in Classical Physics and its Relationship to Light

"The hardest thing to understand in the world is the income tax."
Albert Einstein

I will begin with the scientific understanding of time because it is relatively straightforward to explain. Scientific conclusions often get disproportionately more respect than the conclusions of less formulaic methods because the explanations that result are so detailed. Of course, scientific understanding remains theoretical on many points when dealing with time and the beginning of the universe, and highly disputed when it comes to the realm of quantum mechanics, but that only puts it temporarily on a level field with spirituality and philosophy. In any case, theoretical physics has transformed the discussion of time and light into a modern art, and it would be a shame not to appreciate it.

Naturally, any discussion of light and time must begin with the theory of relativity, if not more basic ideas like Newton's laws of motion, which I will assume is familiar to the reader. Physics can be divided into two categories – classical, which will be discussed in this section, and quantum mechanics, of which some elements will be examined in the following section. Classical physics begins with Newton, continues through the work of Einstein, and includes the aforementioned theory of relativity. Quantum mechanics developed fully in the twentieth century, and challenges many of the ideas in classical physics and introduced the importance of our observation on, for instance, the state of electrons. At many points, the details that follow are primarily derived from the work and lectures of Stephen Hawking and the late Richard Feynman, since the clear and concise explanations they gave have made this topic accessible to the public.

The conclusions of physics are presented here not because they relate directly to the material presented in the sections that follow – those sections deal with time's interaction with the human condition, and not about time itself – but rather because it is an excellent example of how knowledge can increase the number of possibilities we can consider. By learning more about time as presented by physics, we open ourselves to a wide range of ideas, some of which will be outlined later in this section. Similarly, when we learn more about anything, we gain greater perspective on that area, and have greater confidence when dealing with matters in that area. As an example of how to gain perspective on the conditions of life, and how time might interact with those conditions, it is fitting that we start with an attempt to gain broader perspective on time itself.

An explanation of relativity is straightforward in that there is really only one way to explain it with any clarity, not because it is necessarily easy to understand. It is absolutely necessary for an understanding of time itself, however, so there is no avoiding the need to explain it. Relativity was originally stated by Newton, and essentially says that when bodies are together, say in a vehicle of some sort, then everything inside the vehicle will seem to be at rest so long as the vehicle is traveling at constant speed – there should be no way to tell that the vehicle is moving. Think about being in the back seat of a car and looking outside the window. It seems like the rest of the world is moving in the opposite direction. Technically, there is every reason for you to believe that the car is in fact standing still, and it is instead the rest of the world that is moving – at least, you can believe this as long as you travel at a constant speed. If the car accelerates or decelerates, then it becomes obvious that it was in fact the car that was moving. Such acceleration is considered a change in the inertial frame of reference of the car. While traveling at a constant speed, the car was (in an ideal and purely simplified sense) moving on inertia, and therefore was in a constant frame of reference in relation to the universe. When it changed speeds, the car shifted to a new frame of reference. It will be important to remember for the discussion ahead that we determine what is moving by examining which object has changed reference frames.

Let's say that, from the backseat of the car, you threw a ball onto the dashboard at a speed of twenty miles an hour while the car was moving at sixty miles an hour. Now, for you, the ball was only traveling at twenty miles an hour. In fact, if the ball could have felt how fast it was going, it would have measured its own speed at twenty miles an hour. However, take the point of view of someone on the sidewalk watching your car whiz by. For that person on the sidewalk, the ball would have been traveling eighty miles an hour – the sixty mile an hour speed of the car added to the twenty mile an hour speed of the ball. In relation to the frame of reference held by the person from the sidewalk, anything moving in the car should be subject to this adding of speeds. Back in the car, though, you know very well that you cannot throw at eighty miles an hour. For one thing, the ball would have gone right over the dashboard and smashed the windshield at that speed, but it didn't. This difference in observed phenomena, dependant on the observer's inertial frame of reference, is called relativity.

Under normal circumstances, this alone poses no problem. There is one fact that Newton had no way of knowing, though – light in a vacuum travels at the speed c, which is equal to

300000 km/sec, and that speed is a universal constant. Let's say that someone is traveling in a spaceship at a velocity of 150000 km/sec, then measures the speed of the light passing through a vacuum tube within his ship. His measurement must show that light is traveling at c – 300000 km/sec – since it is a constant. If his measurement was different, then he would know he was moving, and that would violate relativity. However, let us see what is happening from the vantage point of an observer outside the spacecraft. In the case of the ball in the car, we simply added velocities. We can do so here – adding the spaceship's speed of 150000 km/sec to light's speed of 300000 km/sec – but we get 450000 km/sec, which is impossible. The observer cannot be seeing light traveling faster than c, since that would violate the universal constant of the speed of light in a vacuum. Nor can we abandon relativity. For instance, let's say that instead of traveling at its full speed, the light seemed to be traveling at 150000 km/sec within the ship because, combined with the speed of the spacecraft itself, that would look to be 300000 km/sec to the outside observer. In other words, let's say that we subtracted speeds instead of adding them. But that would mean that the ball in the car, instead of flying forward at twenty miles an hour, would actually fly into your face at forty miles an hour – negative forty miles an hour in relation to the motion of the car. We all know from experience in a moving vehicle that that is not the case. We can all testify that, under normal circumstances, relativity is correct. The resolution of the problem of light's relation to relativity leads to the modern conception of time as understood by physics.

There's no need to go into every particular of the experiments and the logic taken to solve this problem, not to mention other issues that led to Einstein's special theory of relativity, since only the implications of the solution concern this discussion. The Special Theory of Relativity, formulated

On the Nature of Time

by Einstein, states that the astronaut will not notice anything, and in his view light will be going at its full speed – 300000 km/sec. However, if someone observing from Earth was able to note the behavior of light in the spacecraft, it will seem to him that the light inside the spacecraft was going at the speed of light as well – not 450000 km/sec. Naturally, this discrepancy had to be resolved, but it took a genius of Einstein's capabilities to manage it, and it would take a few physics lectures to understand it. To simplify the explanation, approaching the speed of light actually distorts the length of the spacecraft. Everything in the spacecraft, including rulers and the astronaut's own body, is shortened in the direction of motion so that light within the vessel actually has less apparent distance to travel, though since the astronaut's ruler is also shortened, his vessel seems to be its full length – otherwise he would be able to tell by the length of his vessel how fast he was going. For the observer on Earth, of course, there is no such shortening, which is why he sees the light going at 300000 km/sec, not 450000 km/sec – in other words, slower than it should be going. If this is difficult to understand, don't worry. After laying down some more concepts, there will be an example of how it works and further discussion.

Before going into the example, we need to see how the behavior of light might influence time, which is our primary focus. Imagine if a clock that used the speed of light to determine time was fitted into the spacecraft, perhaps calibrated while at rest to measure a second every time a particle of light crossed the midpoint between two mirrors. For the astronaut, time would have to be proceeding at the normal pace according to the clock, since by the rules of relativity light has to be apparently going at its normal pace. On the other hand, if the observer on Earth was able to see the clock, he would think that the astronaut's clock was slow. This would have to be true of all clocks regardless of whether they were mechanical or based on radioactive decay, or oriented in directions other than in the direction of motion, because otherwise the astronaut would be able to tell he was moving because of the difference between those clocks and the clock based on light. And everything about the astronaut has to be consistent with this – including his breathing and aging – otherwise he would be able to use the discrepancy between those things and the clock to tell that he was moving.

One way we can tell that this is the case is because certain particles – muons - have definite, and short, lifetimes. At rest, their lifetimes are measurable and lie within a clear range. However, when traveling at close to the speed of light, muons travel much farther than they should be able to at that speed. In other words, their lifetimes appear to us longer when they travel at close to the speed of light. From the point of view of the particles themselves, they had their normal short lifetimes. It is the time dilation of objects traveling close to the speed of light that explains this discrepancy.

Now for an example that will hopefully make things clear. Suppose that there is a person in a spacecraft – we'll call her S – and someone on Earth – called E. We'll say S is already traveling at $0.99c$ – just under the speed of light – and as she passes by Earth, synchronizes her watch with E. In addition to this, S will emit a flash of light from the back of her ship every one of her seconds so that E can keep track of the discrepancy between their watches. As S flies away from Earth at $0.99c$, it seems to E that the flashes of light occur only once every fourteen seconds. It is important to remember that the time dilation factor for an object traveling at $0.99c$ is a factor of 7 – this is derived from an equation that will be discussed further on. In other words, E is actually aging seven times faster than S. What about the other way around? After all, isn't E going away from S at $0.99c$? Why isn't the reciprocal about them true? In fact, if S could see E, it would seem that

On the Nature of Time

E was actually aging seven times slower. This is simply due to the increased time light takes to close the gap between S and E. In fact, E is aging much faster, but the only way for us to tell this is if E and S come back together on Earth.

So, let's say that S's journey is a one year journey out from Earth, and a one year journey back. During this journey, E will see that the flashes occur once every fourteen seconds out, and fourteen times every second when the spacecraft turns back towards Earth. That's right, E will actually see S's clock run fast on the journey back. However, take a closer look at the factors. On the outbound year, E will have aged fourteen years while S will have aged one. On the inbound year, E will have aged less than a month while S will have aged a year. In total, then, E will have aged a little more than fourteen years while S will have aged two years. That is where we get the time dilation factor of seven – fourteen divided by two.

According to E, S turned the spaceship around after seven years at a distance of just under seven light years (S was traveling at 0.99c, so naturally she would have traveled seven light years in seven years). However, E notes that he only saw the turn around after fourteen years since the light from the turn around itself took seven years to cover the distance back from the event. For S, however, she only traveled for one year, so she only covered what was, to her, 0.99 light years. Remember that distance is shortened in the direction of motion when a vehicle gets closer to the speed of light? That's what happened in this case to S – by a factor of 7.

There are many problems that need to be explained. First, when did E age? According to S's calculations, E was actually aging slowly – by a factor of 7 – on the outbound year, and slowly by the same factor on the inbound year. That's just under two months for each of S's years, or a grand total of four months. So, at what point did E age the rest of the fourteen years? It's on the turn around. You see, when S turned around, she decelerated, which means she changed her inertial frame of reference. And, just like in a car, you are allowed to know that you have moved when you change your frame of reference. So, according to S's calculations, E would have suddenly aged all thirteen years and eight months during S's turnaround, when she changed her frame of reference. What S actually saw was that E aged thirteen years and ten months on the inbound year. If S had never turned around, and continued traveling at 0.99c away from Earth, she would have seen E age ten years when she aged seventy. In actuality, though, by the time S was seventy, E would have been hundreds of years dead – a fact S would only know if she turned around and headed all the way back.

Hopefully, this provides some explanation for the workings of time dilation thanks to special relativity. Notice that it unifies space and time – length itself was relative, just like time was. What for S was a single light year in distance, was for E seven light years. What for S was one year in time, was for E seven years. When physicists talk of the fabric of space-time, it might be confusing to those who, in regular life, have always thought of space and time separately. As shown in this example, though, all four dimensions are just a single fabric, with their nature dependent on an observer's inertial reference frame.

Aside from the affect on length in the direction of motion, experiments showed another change when an object approached the speed of light. This one concerns mass, particularly in the equation force equals mass times acceleration (F=ma). Newton had assumed that mass is constant, while in fact it increases as a body approaches the speed of light. The adjusted equation for mass, which was Einstein's main contribution to the resolution of this problem, is that: m (moving mass) = mass at rest / sqrt($1 - v^2/c^2$). The normal car travels at 30 meters per second (around 67 miles and hour), while c is 300,000,000 meters per second, so v^2/c^2 is, for the average car, infinitesimal. So, when that number is subtracted from one, and then square-rooted, the result is so close to one that the effect is immeasurable. However, if a spacecraft was traveling at 0.9c, then division of the squares would result in 0.81, and the denominator after the square root would be 0.44. If a person with a mass of fifty kilograms at rest traveled at 0.9c, that person's mass at that velocity would inflate to almost 114 kilograms. Of course, the person would not notice this increase in weight, otherwise he would be able to tell that he was moving. This alternation in the equation also implies that matter cannot reach the speed of light – because its mass will steadily increase to infinity. This also eventually leads to special relativity's relation to gravity, which is what the General Theory of Relativity by Einstein discusses. Gravity is shown to distort the space-time fabric. Incidentally, to get the time dilation factor created by velocities close to the speed of light, simply plug in 1 for mass at rest and the velocity for v in the equation, and the result will be the factor. For instance, making v = 0.99c will result in a denominator of 0.1414, and dividing 1 by 0.1414 gives a time dilation factor of 7, as applied in the S and E example.

The point is that time, not to mention length and mass, is dependant on a person's frame of reference. Also, a person's perspective is limited by the speed of light, as time itself is. While most of the discussion will revolve around perceptions of time, the nature of time itself can provide valuable clues as to how we should think of it. For instance, isn't the idea that the astronaut in the spaceship might live thousands of Earth years enticing? Of course, it should not be, since the astronaut will still only experience a normal lifespan, but there is still an underlying desire to cheat time. The more a person learns about relativity, the more intriguing ideas get.

But there is more to theoretical physics' examination of time, especially in the concept of space-time. A point in the four dimensional fabric of space-time is called an event, and that event has a past and a future. In this past, there is a cone expanding behind it that indicates the possible events in the past that might have affected the event, while in the future there is another cone, indicating those events that might be affected by this event. Space-time diagrams of this sort are useful to get a grasp of all sorts of phenomena, even the example of S and E presented above. However, the examination of the past and future implicit in such a diagram is of interest all on its own, in a philosophical rather than purely physical manner. At one point, Richard Feynman indicated that "now" has no definite meaning, since due to what we have already learned about light and relativity, now is only what past actions have affected. In the context of the discussion here, "now" should be understood not so much by looking from the past to the present, but instead by looking at the present into the future to find a definition – in which case "now" is when we can create the affective future. This is a preferable understanding because, as active entities interacting with the universe instead of passive observers analyzing it, we have more of an interest in the way the future will turn out. We can leave that issue – it is enough to understand the concepts of events, the affective past, and the affective future, and to understand that these cones, and the ability of one event to cause or change another, are limited by the speed of light.

For physics in the twentieth century, the clearest goal of all of this is to figure out what happened at the beginning of the universe, if it had a beginning. The main method of achieving this goal through physics is to develop a unified theory which will combine the four main physical forces – gravitation, electromagnetic, strong nuclear, and weak nuclear. Currently the main hurdle is to reconcile classical physics with quantum mechanics. Beginnings can tell much, if not everything, about how something works. Not coincidentally, spiritual systems also have an interest in the start of the universe, mainly because they also theorize about how the universe works, and are just as protective of those theories. Spirituality rarely explicitly discusses time, though, while science has done quite a thorough job of it. Science can actually shed some light on the usually cryptic creation stories from various cultures and religions. So, let us move beyond what is provable by science, and take a look at some assumptions that might follow from it.

All of space-time is part of the universe, so if there was a Big Bang in which the universe originated from a single point, all time should also have expanded from that point. In fact, if anything lies outside of the universe, we are completely incapable of interacting with it, at least in the form we are currently in and with the perception of time we currently have. Most creation myths show some understanding of what the beginning of the universe might have been like, but interestingly most of them contain a clear sense that time was in an infant state. In the Genesis, God had a six-day creation. It may have been metaphorical, or it might have been to show the power of God, but either way it is interesting that such definite time should be cited. Indian cosmology is far more explicit – Brahma creates the universe in one of his days, which is equal to about eight billion years. Brahma's life lasts a hundred of his years, and in the cosmology that represents the entire lifetime of the universe. These are only the more recognizable of the creation stories that show time passing for a deity at a slower rate, but to claim anything more than an interesting coincidence at this point would be overstating things.

Taking a good look at the beginning of the universe as physicists present it, a few questions present themselves. First, assuming that there was a Big Bang, and that all time originated from that point, does that mean that everything that will ever happen in the universe, occurred at that point? In a strict sense, everything that has occurred was at least predetermined at that point. Consider the Big Bang as an event, for instance, and everything that came out of it is necessarily in its affective future. This is obvious from common sense, but also when looking at a space-time diagram, setting the Big Bang as the event, and noting that the cone of the affective future must include the universe. But if time is merely another dimension, and we can be certain that all space is just an expansion from that point, getting thinner as it spreads out, why can't time have all been played out right there, and be simply spreading out to fulfill itself? In fact, the Big Bang technically defies the limit of causality – at one point it probably exceeded the speed of light. It is likely that the initial inflation of the universe actually exceeded the speed of light. This is possible because it is not something in the universe traveling, but rather space itself spreading out. There are no speed limits on the spread of space. But perhaps space only seems spread out because we are here to observe it – a possibility that will be examined further in the chapter on quantum mechanics. Time may be apparently progressing, but perhaps it simply takes longer for us to realize that something has already happened as space-time gets stretched.

The implications might determine to what extent we have free will. If all time had been present at the start of the universe, and the course of the universe determined right at the Big Bang because it was the sole event that would determine all else that could occur in the universe, then all actions within this universe were predetermined at that point. So, how can we claim to have any sort of free will? The exercise of free will would imply that we are somehow above the universe; that the part of us with free will actually originated from the level of the creation, outside of the universe, not inside the universe.

On the Nature of Time

Also, I find the possibility intriguing, and in this I am definitely not the first, that this universe all developed and we all live our lives in that primordial particle of creation. In other words, that it might have expanded from our point of view, but from outside this universe, it is still that particle. Some have proposed that our universe is merely a blade of grass in another universe. After all, if our time does not occur outside the universe, and the entire development of the universe has occurred through the time dimension of this universe, this development cannot be perceived by those outside the universe. The outside is beyond space and time, or at least our version of space-time. This musing, of course, assumes an outside set of dimensions. In this outside set of dimensions there may be other ways to perceive things that we cannot imagine.

So, we have taken a cursory look at relativity and space-time. Space-time is dynamic, as can be seen from the ways length, time, and mass are no longer constant when a body approaches the speed of light. The General Theory of Relativity explains that gravity distorts space-time, conceptually creating an indentation in the fabric so that a large mass will pull smaller masses into it. A black hole, a mass of infinite density at a single point, is often depicted as a cone-shaped indentation in space-time in which even light cannot escape. But in what dimension does a black hole puncture the fabric? Imagine that a piece of paper is perfectly two dimensional, and you can see that any crinkle or fold in it has to be in a third dimension. Anything with sufficient mass will create an indentation in space-time in a similar way, and black holes have extreme mass at a single point, so they make drastic indentations. How many dimensions are there? String theory, which is currently physics' best bet for discovering the unified theory, suggests that ten is a possibility in five separate theories, eleven required for a unification of those five theories, and twenty-six not unlikely. For those who have trouble enough keeping track of the usual four, don't worry, the rest are mentioned only to suggest some unexpected possibilities.

For instance, moving fully away from physics and toward spirituality, it is at once obvious that, assuming that there was a creator or creative force at the beginning of the universe, then either the creator was completely outside of the universe, the universe is a part of this creator, or the creator is the universe. The very idea that there are many more dimensions than we can immediately perceive makes the first and second possibilities as likely as the third, whereas without this knowledge, the idea that the creator is the universe would be easily the most likely. To put it coarsely, it is a question of where to place God, or any pantheon of deities. While simply assuming a few extra dimensions outside of the universe might seem unreasonable, there is no other way to go about it. As long as we are a part of this universe, we have no way of looking outside to prove any theories. Since, in this case, "outside" means whatever might exist other than our universe, and we will never be able to interact with it, science cannot help to prove things either way.

Regardless of which of the three models of a creator we might actually have, if any, there is one thing that should be clear. If this universe was created by some deity or conscious force, that creator must have been capable of seeing all time instantaneously, such that the past, present, and future was undifferentiated, because otherwise the creator would not have been able to fashion space-time. Without that, the creator must have created the universe by accident, because it certainly would not have been able to perceive it. I would consider a creator incapable of traveling at the speed of light a huge letdown, since that would show an inability to transcend matter, and would prefer one that could not only reach but also pass the speed of light – which would entail a transcendence of time. This transcendence of time that should be expected from any creator of the universe can be called the universal level of consciousness, and it can apply to either the creating deity or a consciousness underlying the universe itself. The key characteristics of this consciousness are that it can perceive an eternal now, and to the extent that it can travel, it can at least reach the speed of light. If such a consciousness exists, then perhaps the four main forces of gravitation, electromagnetism, the weak nuclear, and the strong nuclear are like its arms and legs, and the single unified theory physicists are looking for is, in fact, the embryonic mind of the creation. On the other hand, it might be totally different.

In any case, if we can claim at all to have free will, it has to rest at the level of the universal consciousness, otherwise it would be trapped by the fabric of time unleashed by the Big Bang. Whether we can actually exercise our free will while part of the universe is an open question, since it would either mean our free will only applied to those activities that would not change how the rest of the universe proceeded, or we would be actually changing the nature of the Big Bang as we altered the course of things, which is not entirely impossible given the dynamic nature of time, but highly unlikely. It is also possible that the Big Bang never changes, but as we exercise free will we create wild distortions in the way the universe functions, and either the universe itself is adaptable to such changes, or the effects are left unresolved.

It is easy to get frustrated with all the "ifs", various possibilities, and the complete conditional nature of so many ideas. Certainty is more comforting and convenient, but as will be emphasized later, people have to find their own way, and discover the correct balances and ways for themselves. Honesty requires that the conditionals should be used, so that there is no illusion that anything unproven is absolute truth.

Anyway, thanks to science we can see that time is a fairly intricate and interesting thing to explore in its own right. There

Time and the Human Condition

is still much for researchers to delve into. Meanwhile, after a look quantum mechanics, we can take a closer look at ideas in areas that defy rigid proofs, and see how time involves itself in spirituality and everyday life.

On the Nature of Time

Perspective and Quantum Mechanics

"For every human problem, there is a neat, simple solution; and it is always wrong."
H. L. Mencken

Initially, I had only planned one section on physics because quantum mechanics, though certainly having some interesting ideas, focuses more on the smaller elements of the way the universe works while classical physics has more of an eye on the cosmic level. As it turns out, the details are every bit as important as the big picture. Quantum physics focuses in on light and small particles, like electrons, in an examination of the workings of the universe at this fundamental level. Where it has most diverged from classical physics is its emphasis on probability, which Einstein disliked, and the presence of instantaneous influence in the theory, which violates the speed of light limit. The initial choice to ignore quantum physics was abandoned upon an examination of Bell's theorem, which is profound in its possible implications and highly debated, and therefore attracts the curiosity of anyone seeking perspectives on the universe.

Bell's theorem was meant to address Einstein's criticisms of quantum mechanics (hereafter QM), which were centered on the way QM required instantaneous transfer of information and probability. Einstein, Podolsky, and Rosen published what is known as the EPR paradox, a thought experiment that showed QM violated locality – which demands that separate systems in space cannot have instantaneous affects on one another, and are limited by the speed of light as shown by special relativity. At issue is the spin of electron pairs, and the way they apparently always have opposing spins. Instead of somehow instantaneously communicating spin to each other, it is possible that there exists a hidden variable that determines spin ahead of time. That hidden variable would be what is missing in quantum mechanics, according to Einstein.

The problem with hidden variables is that there would have to be an infinite number of them – one for each possible axis along which the electron might spin, since the opposing spin of the electrons works with any measurement taken. The achievement of John Stewart Bell was to develop an inequality with three different measurements, and three possible hidden variables, that any theory attempting to defy QM and resolve the observed phenomenon must satisfy. Bell's theorem is that, if actual measurements of spin do not satisfy the inequality, then it is violated and, thanks to proof by negation, one of the three assumptions of the inequality must be false. Using logic to derive the inequality, it can be stated simply as: Number (A, not B) + Number (B, not C) greater than or equal to Number (A, not C), with A, B, and C being our three different measurements of spin (this version of the inequality was taken from a document by David M. Harrison of the University of Toronto, whose explanation of Bell's theorem was consulted to develop my own views on it). The inequality itself assumes two basic things – that logic is valid, and that the parameters A, B, and C have an existence independent of measurement, being part of a reality separate from the influence of the observer. Applied to electrons, the inequality also assumes locality – the speed of light limit for causality, by necessity of previous discoveries in physics. Since the theorem is a proof by negation, it anticipates that one of these three assumptions is actually false, which would answer the EPR paradox by poking a hole in local realism and refuting one of Einstein's cherished views of the operation of the universe.

QM, of course, violates the inequality, predicting values that would not satisfy it. The main contribution of this is that the actual experiments performed match the predictions of QM, and also violate the inequality. Assuming that there are no flaws in Bell's theorem, the violation of the inequality means that at least one of three assumptions it was based on is false. The basic assumption is that logic is valid, a necessary assumption for any proof based on negation. The next is the presence of hidden variables, and the final assumption is locality. So either logic is not valid, or there is no hidden variable, or information – some physicists insist that information is incorrect, and that the term "influence" should be used instead, so I will use it from here on since the change is subtle and reasonable – can be passed faster than the speed of light. Let's take these one at a time, starting with the last.

If locality has to be abandoned, this creates a problematic situation, since every particle in the universe would be capable of it and all theories produced assuming the speed of light as a limit would have to be reconsidered. I do not know how far research has gone in this direction, but having considered the possibilities, there is one interesting idea that might be proposed. We have already discussed that there are dimensions in excess of the four space-time dimensions, which are part of string theory, and perhaps another set outside of the universe in which the universe was formed. The first thing to note is that string theory, by adding dimensions, is trying to address Bell's theorem and unify classical physics and quantum mechanics. So far, however, string theory is not widely accepted. On the other hand, this universe may have the limit of locality, but whatever plane the creation occurred in is almost certainly capable of instantaneous influence, since anything else would require time to be a dimension outside the universe.

The possibility that human beings are capable of communication, and eventually expanding our consciousness, to reach the eternal now has been noted. But what if every electron was also capable of receiving influence from that plane? The possibility is very appealing, and may be related to another question – was the creation a single event, or did the creator leave within the universe ways by which he could alter it after the initial creation. If the creation was a single event, then there would be no need for particles to communicate with the universal consciousness. But if the creation is an ongoing process, or if the creator left it open to be one, then there would have to be a way for the plane of the universal consciousness to influence the matter of the universe. This is not very scientific, but certainly worth thinking about. As far as physics goes, string theory and its ten, eleven, or twenty-six dimensions is probably the best bet for a unified theory.

Now let us move to the abandonment of hidden variables, which is even more abstract in its implications. QM has always had an uneasy relationship with traditional ideas of reality. Consider Heisenberg's Uncertainty Principle, for instance, and his statement that the path of the electron comes into existence only when we observe it. The idea of hidden variables tried to explain this away by suggesting that there are simply variables that we are not aware of which determine the path of the electron ahead of time. Or, in the case of the EPR paradox and Bell's inequality, it is the spin of the electron. If the hidden variable idea is abandoned, then our participation in the universe has a fundamental impact on it – which is not entirely a surprise. However, does this mean we can finally answer the question about whether the tree that falls in the woods with nobody there makes a sound? Is the answer "no"? The ultimate conclusion is that there is no reality separate from observation, which is taking things to extremes. This corresponds with philosophical idealism (which bears some relationship to political idealism, but for clarity should not be confused with it), which posits that thought is fundamental reality. This opposes philosophical realism, which is defined exactly as scientific realism is – that the universe exists independent of observation.

In the former discussion about classical physics, it was noted that human free will would require either the creation of the universe itself to change, or the universe would somehow have to adapt to the presence of beings with true free will. The elasticity of reality may be the universe's way of adapting. If the whole universe was already determined at its start, it is also possible that the observation of the universe forced it to expand in order to play itself out. In other words, the universe is still the event point, but because we are within the universe and part of it, it seems to us to have the expanded time and space. The universe only exists in this form because it is observing itself through species like us. Therefore, none of it is independent as long as beings with limited consciousness, and moment-by-moment awareness, observe it.

That's a difficult way to look at things, and physicist and philosophers have endeavored to explain the situation in terms of self-reference, which also connects to the possibility that logic is invalid. In 1931, Gödel proved that logic is at least incomplete by using self-reference. The main reason why the assumption that logic is valid must be made in relation to Bell's theorem is because Bell proves his point by the negation of the inequality. According to logic, either something is true or false – so, if something is not true, it must be false. The problem is that this might not be the case, particularly in a situation involving self-reference. Take the paradoxical statement "This statement is false" for instance. It is either both true and false or neither – an affect made possible by the way it refers to itself. Whether this has any bearing on Bell's theorem hinges on whether it is a case of self-reference. When we make observations about the universe, is it a case of the universe referring to itself? If so, then perhaps this flaw in logic is enough to deny proof by negation to Bell's theorem. This does not mean that locality and the hidden variable are somehow safe, just that Bell has been denied logic as a means of proving his point. Which leaves the question – what recourse do we have to prove it, then?

On the other hand, simply because we are the universe and we are referring to it does not mean that proof by negation will cause a paradox. If I say, "this statement is a lie," it defies logic, but if I say "I am six feet tall," then that statement is either true or false, and is not paradoxical. Bell's inequality has more chance of being the latter than the former, but the gap is enough to ensure the theorem cannot completely prove its point – assuming this is a case of self-reference. Even if the theorem holds, it is possible that self-reference can contribute to the issue of hidden variables. By observing and participating in the universe, we have an impact on it. This idea has been fleshed out by J.A. Wheeler, who compared the idea to two mirrors facing each other and producing seemingly infinite reflections.

So the refutation of any of the three assumptions of Bell's inequality – the validity of logic, hidden variables creating a universe independent of observation, and locality – would result in unique consequences for science and philosophy. Continuing successes in the area of quantum mechanics will no doubt bring even more interesting ideas and, despite the objections of Einstein, it looks like it is still going strong and capable of predicting phenomena that classical physics cannot explain. Unfortunately, it does not have the neatness and intuitive sense that classical physics had to recommend it. In both politics and philosophy, realism is always easier to grasp, and therefore immediately attractive. Instead, quantum

On the Nature of Time

mechanics shows us a universe that is counterintuitive, a universe that might alter itself at our slightest glance. But perhaps, as H.L. Mencken said in the quote at the start of this section, the neat, simple answer is wrong.

Time and the Human Condition

The Ability to Contemplate Eternity is Not a Survival Trait

Having discussed physics, it will be interesting to discuss another scientific idea that has bearing on the development of humanity and the human condition over time – evolution. Evolution is a characteristic of the physical universe, and describes how life has developed on Earth over time, and so should not be seen as conflicting with the potential for higher levels of consciousness. Higher levels of consciousness should lie beyond the physical universe. It is sometimes assumed to be in conflict, but that is a matter of cultural interference in spirituality – a frequent problem that will be discussed deeply in the sections that follow. The body, along with the physical attributes of the brain, evolves. But by evolution alone there is a limit to the extent human consciousness can reach. The wider limit is set by the universe – the human consciousness cannot transcend time or the speed of light. The narrow limit is set by evolution itself, which sets the limit at what fulfills the practical needs of the human race – what makes humanity more fit to survive. The interesting thing is that, logically, we have already surpassed the practical needs of our species, which lends hope to the further development of our consciousness up to the limit set by the universe. Unlike any other creature we know of, we can contemplate, if not see or understand, eternity. We consider the beginning of the universe, the end of the universe, and what happens to beings after they die, even if we hold no specific beliefs in any area. This capability shows the extent of human ingenuity, and our great geniuses are often those who probe into the farthest reaches.

The survival of the fittest is often associated with evolution, though it need not be. It is only one model of how evolution might function. But the ability to adapt to one's environment the best, and to therefore increase chances of procreation and passing on genes to the next generation, seems to be a logical and orderly explanation for what would otherwise be a haphazard evolutionary process. The thing is, the universe can sometimes be counterintuitive. Quantum mechanics' contradiction of local realism, with realism being intuitively reasonable to almost everyone living within the universe and who has ever kicked a rock, is a prime example of how the universe might not work in a straightforward manner. Because of the limits of human intuition, an explanation can make sense yet still be questioned, and that questioning can deal with the assumptions of evolution as much as it might attack classical physics. Survival of the fittest is, however, the key to evolution as we understand it today.

Our ability to contemplate eternity, though, is not a survival trait, and nor does it provide any distinct benefit to our ability to procreate. In fact, given the profound and time-consuming thoughts that thinking about eternity inspires, it might actually tend to hinder procreation. Certainly, that was the explicit understanding and intention in the Catholic Church with the vow of celibacy – without that vow, those in the church would be not be spending all their time contemplating the eternal and the divine. The fact that we think about the afterlife, and times beyond our own lifespan, is absolutely essential for the development of spirituality and the more abstract areas of imagination (as opposed to basic imagination, which is the direct product of observation and reflection), which are also not survival traits. That level of thought is also the window by which we can gain perspective and see what it is we lack – the ability to fully transcend time.

Perhaps contemplating eternity is a byproduct of more essential functions our mind provides, and while providing no genetic advantage, it also provides no disadvantage. The basic level of our imagination, after all, is required for survival. It has allowed us to develop and use tools, compensating for our lack of physical strength compared to other creatures our size. But even if it was merely the byproduct of our imagination, the widespread presence of higher thought and its persistence generation after generation is quite remarkable, and suggests that the ability is important rather than just being an accident. It is difficult to consider the contemplation of eternity in the same terms as we might speak of the appendix – a leftover from an earlier phase of evolution that should be surgically removed if it causes any problems or gets infected – but it leads to implications that will be discussed further on.

The broader perspective the human race has thanks to this ability has resulted in many tendencies that actually move the species in a direction contrary to what evolution defines as most productive. In Europe, the centuries long cultural taboo against sex before marriage and the way procreation is delayed despite the fact that the physical capability is present at an early age are both justified by religious restriction, but developed in their most extreme form in the Victorian era, when the culture developed the meaning of 'civilization' and what it means to be 'civilized'. Laws against teen pregnancy persist because they are perceived as being beneficial for society. Nevertheless, all of this is contrary to the survival of the fittest, as are the more compassionate measures in the laws of society, and by all logic, the societies that do not have such laws should overrun those that do. Instead, of course, the European societies that had such rules were better able to organize themselves, as a demographic response to both better healthcare and increasing urbanization, and became more successful. But the Europeans would never have even developed the theories to make the demographic shift if they only obeyed survival of the fittest, and lacked the ability to consider a stretch of time beyond their own lives.

It should be noticed, though, that we are steadily abandoning this sort of foresight. Consider the way we deal with the environment and fossil fuels as a key example. Clearly, we occasionally make steps in the right direction, but given the magnitude of the problem, the foresight of our leaders in the United States today is nowhere near the level of, say, the framers of the Constitution, despite the fact that we have more knowledge, supposedly better education, and information resources that are almost light-speed accessible thanks to the internet. So whatever our physical evolution, and our technological development, we are actually regressing as far as higher consciousness is concerned – at least on the small scale of the past century. Perhaps if we develop a cultural taboo against the use of depleting fossil fuels, with a possible supplementary reason being that the fuel is actually composed of long dead creatures, people would make more effort and provide more research funding toward alternates.

Our ability to contemplate eternity can also be used to define sentience. There are probably more scientific definitions, though these are debatable since we know of only one sentient species, so there is no basis for comparison. The reason why this ability should provide a good dividing line between sentience and non-sentience is purely because it is necessary for higher level of understanding and more complex organization of society to develop. Developing levels of understanding beyond those strictly beneficial to survival and procreation certainly marks the human race as unique among species. In fact, it is the only way we could develop ideas about our uniqueness at all. Without a kind of perspective beyond those defined as survival instincts, a land-bound species would find it impossible to develop artificial flight, much less take to space. Meanwhile, with the extent of eternity waiting for us to explore it, we, as a sentient species, cannot help but launch into it.

Another possibility for why we have a sense of eternity, though one that is rarely considered because we assume a gradual evolution from monkeys to homo sapiens, is that the ability is actually something left over from an earlier stage of evolution. In other words, it is actually like the appendix. Needless to say, this is rarely considered because we are fond of our sentience, and the appendix is only important when it is a hindrance. Regardless of the unpopularity of this view, our ability may have had a very practical use at some earlier point that it no longer has now. It may have been the initial spark that led to all our other cognitive abilities, which made us capable of moving beyond our fellow species. The spark might have been a brief connection to that universal consciousness that lies outside the normal rules and dimensions of this universe, and that initial contact had enough latent influence to carry through to today, and make so many of us certain that there is a God. For the spiritual, this is a particularly enticing possibility, and certainly explains a great deal. Outside of spirituality, perhaps it would be useful to think of this spark as inspiration, the raw component of creativity.

A more extreme idea, but one that is more often discussed that the one above, is that the physical form of the species developed via evolution, but the spirit and consciousness of humanity actually came into this universe from the outside plane of existence, and simply decided to occupy the forms that were already part of the universe, so that the spirit could more affectively interact with the universe. Certainly, this is in agreement with those belief systems, like Christianity, which show the human race initially capable of communicating with God fairly readily. There is, in many cultures, a sense of a Golden Age in which this communication was easy, meaning that the leap from regular human consciousness to universal consciousness was one everyone knew how to bridge. Eventually, our spirits would have become increasingly accustomed to the physical form, much like water takes the shape of its container. This is essentially the "fall of man" idea, and at this point, being more of an optimist, I prefer the "initial spark" explanation of human sentience.

Part 2
Purpose in Life

Purpose in Life

Basic Possibilities After This Life

What is the meaning or purpose behind life? That is the most popularized 'ultimate question'. The possible answers are actually fairly limited, as are the answers to all questions relating to how people ought to live their lives when those answers are generalized. The problem is that there is no way of determining which answer is correct. We have all sorts of holy figures, both the people themselves and the stories about them, each giving a general proposal and a collection of specifics. Moses, for instance, presented the general covenant between God and humans concerning what would get people into heaven, following an existing belief that there was a heavenly afterlife to could get into. The specifics of Moses' beliefs are the Ten Commandments, and an entire body of mundane laws that are divinely supported, including the eye for eye and tooth for tooth measure of justice. But if the specifics are temporarily ignored – specifics of spiritual systems like what types of meat people should not eat might have practical effects, but they do not address the heart of the ultimate question – the variations are fairly small. This section will examine the set of possible afterlives, and the condition where there isn't one, and briefly describe each one's immediate implications. The following section will deal more specifically with purpose in this life with respect to these possible afterlives, and how they relate to each other.

The figures associated with various religions and spiritual systems all show a clear transcendence of time. Buddha's search for universal consciousness is well recorded, Moses and the figures of Genesis in general could communicate with the divine, Christ knew of his approaching crucifixion and came back from the dead in three days, Mohammed communicated with the divine when writing the Koran, and altogether any leading spiritual figure that does not show similar traits is considered illegitimate. After all, a person could not claim to know the secret to life and the afterlife without having a more finely tuned consciousness than the average human being.

When it comes to the afterlife, there are basically two possibilities: either there is one, or there isn't. If there is an afterlife, there are a number of possibilities for it, six of which will be explained here. The first three assume that there is a single afterlife that we must go to regardless of what we do in life. If the afterlife is independent of this life, then it can either be better than this, in general the same as this, or worse than this. The next option is that there is a dual or triple afterlife – in the manner of Christian theology, among others – and our actions, thoughts, and beliefs in this life have an impact on where we end up. Reincarnation, the condition in which we continually return to this world, is also a potential afterlife. We can assume at least two possible types of reincarnation – permanent and escapable. Escapable reincarnation would be the condition where what we do in this world, over many lifetimes, could eventually lead to a better afterlife, and can in turn branch off into different variations. These are certainly not all the possibilities, and others will be brought up as necessary, but they are the options most commonly discussed or considered.

Here are the cases to be considered:
- A1 – There is an afterlife everybody automatically goes to that is better than this one.

Purpose in Life

- A2 – There is an afterlife everybody automatically goes to that is equal to this one.
- A3 – There is an afterlife everybody automatically goes to that is worse than this one.
- A4 – There is a dualistic or triple afterlife, and this life determines where you go.
- A5 – There is a permanent state of reincarnation
- A6 – There is an escapable state of reincarnation
- B – There is no afterlife.

Let's go through each of these basic options and examine their implications. In Case A1, the best a person can do in this life is to bear through it in preparation for the better afterlife. Unfortunately, this case would almost certainly lead to depression for most people, and without other modifying factors, it would make suicide seem logical. Case A2 is fairly common, and ends up leaving the focus on this life. If the next life will be essentially the same, then a person might as well do the best they can this time around and enjoy him or herself. Of course, there is the possibility of procrastination, but the logic of putting off living an enjoyable life is unfathomable. Any spiritual system that includes the burial of earthly wealth with the dead – as in the Egyptian pyramids, for instance – is a system based on some variation on Case A2.

Case A3 puts even more emphasis on this life, and especially on leaving some legacy here. Ancient Greek beliefs revolved around such an afterlife, and the horrible afterlife ahead of them led the Greeks to emphasize actions in this life heavily. Gaining fame within this lifetime was the most logical pursuit, as seen from the example set by Achilles, who actually abandons immortality for eternal fame in the Trojan War. The epic writer Homer, though, had Odysseus travel to the underworld to meet with the dead Achilles, who expressed regret that he had not chosen immortality over fame. Regular Greeks did not have the choice of immortality, though, so they chose fame. The small collection of city-states subsequently produced more time-honored achievers than nations with a hundred times its population. In short, Cases A1, A2, and A3 create a continuum from which we can derive one simple conclusion – if there is a single inevitable afterlife, then the pleasantness of that afterlife is inversely proportional to the perceived importance of this life.

In the Dual or Multiple Afterlife scenario, it would be logical for a person to do everything to get to the best afterlife. It would make absolutely no sense in taking any action that would hinder this end. The problem is – who decides what it takes to get to the better afterlife? In general, Case A4 gives rise to religion, which forms rules to attain the best end. When people speak of religion, they are talking about a spiritual system that guides a person to the better end of a Case A4 afterlife. 'Spirituality' is a broad term that refers to all belief systems that discuss elements outside the realm of this life, including all cases in category A.

Case A5 is, at first, the same as A2, with the exception that it implies a perpetual afterlife rather than just one, or a few. Perpetual reincarnation can result in many life goals – ranging from hedonism to charity, and every other set of absolute contrasts. It provides no clear impulse to do anything, and so might as well be left without further discussion. It makes all courses reasonable.

Case A6, then, is the more common way to conceive of reincarnation. It introduces an exit, and therefore makes actions in this life important. As with Case A4, this means there have to be ways by which a person can escape reincarnation. However, unlike A4, this case cannot lead to the structures that define religion. There is a lack of urgency – there is no need to reach the better afterlife through the actions of a single lifetime. People who believe in Case A6, then, cannot be led by a religious structure determining the rules which will lead them to the better end. They have many lifetimes to sort things out, and the attitude this produces does not lend itself to strong religious institutions that will dictate belief without opposition. The first impulse of the priestly class in societies that believe in escapable reincarnation, then, is to impose a dual afterlife – a Case A4 view – on the existing system in order to gain greater influence. This may stem from an earnest intention to prevent people from straying too far from the ideal course. The imposition of the dual afterlife onto an existing escapable reincarnation system did occur in India, and explains why the Brahmin caste, the natural priestly class in that society, was able to gain the influence and develop the hierarchy that it did.

Before moving on, some variety should be introduced to the discussion to give added perspective. One other possibility for an afterlife that does not fit in the discussion as it stands is an intermediate state. An intermediate state is a period of variable length that lies between proper lifetimes. It is theoretically possible that, in such a case, choices that can affect the future of the soul might be made, and that the quality of those choices might be affected by actions in this life. There are two broad situations that might occur in this state: either it is self-contained and is not affected by our actions in this life, in which case it will have no further bearing on the discussion, or it is affected, in which case its status is dependant on the nature of the afterlife that it leads to. So, I have excluded the various versions of the intermediate state from the discussion.

Another complication that should be noted is the afterlife after the first afterlife. With the exception of reincarnation, there is no consideration here concerning what happens after the immediate afterlife, despite the possibility that it might determine what the best course in this life should be. Of course, the reason for it is the fact that people rarely consider matters so far ahead, and it would complicate things needlessly to take the discussion all the way to the ultimate end, whatever that might be.

After looking at the basic consequences of the various afterlives, the case in which there is no afterlife, Case B, has to be taken into account. Since afterlives A2, A3, and A5 essentially put emphasis on this life – making the purpose of this life contained within its own bounds – the meaning of life produced by them are the same as it is for Case B. In other words, half of the possible afterlives should make no logical difference at all. Case B is also important to analyze because, on a day-to-day basis, most people function without thinking much about the afterlife at all, regardless of whether they believe there is one. People generally act in accordance with the most logical course if Case B was true – they simply try to live this life in the best way and the greatest comfort as possible, which is usually stated as to seek pleasure and to avoid pain. When the Declaration of Independence declared that the pursuit of happiness was an inalienable right, it made this claim because it is the natural purpose of life, irrespective of any beliefs about the afterlife, which the American theorists felt was up to the freedom of conscience of the individual.

Since religion is not an issue in Case B, people cannot rely on external structures to determine how to live their lives. However, when groups of people live in close proximity together, they tend to create semi-uniform views, or at least some sort of baseline understanding, without which continual strife would result. Any set of such views can be called a culture, or a subculture if the group that adheres to it also follows a broader set of guidelines within a larger society. The guidelines themselves are cultural norms, and can be anything from clothing to artistic to agricultural to spiritual norms. The community sets its own standards to prevent strife.

To sort out the myriad cultures that people follow, their characteristics can be analyzed using a number of continuums. Two in particular stand out as most important: that between novelty and tradition, and that between freedom and safety. The first continuum will be discussed in the section on the attraction of the new and polarization of the old, and the second will be examined in the sections on government and law. Whether a culture is urban or rural is also essential, since the urban environment fosters diversity of culture, while the rural emphasizes uniformity and mutual support. It should be noted that culture does not enforce or demand the idea that there isn't an afterlife, but simply develops to manage those times when we aren't single-mindedly focused on the spiritual path. In those times, the most natural thing to do is work toward the immediate goals of this life, and to satisfy the needs of the community as a whole.

The cultural way of life is set in contrast to the spiritual only for clarity, and they in fact coincide much of the time. They have to, otherwise the spiritual side of a society would reject the cultural, or vice versa. This sort of rejection, of course, has happened and will happen. For those who believe fully in Case B, then, it is logical to pay great attention to culture, and to make a careful choice of which culture to belong to, since the logical purpose in life would be to live it in the best manner possible, and culture determines one's environment.

Without coming to any conclusions about which spiritual views happen to be right, it is easy to see that the logical courses to take in life are actually fairly limited, as long as they are defined broadly. The specifics are what cause all the conflicts and the tough choices. Summarizing the broad choices, the most common is to simply live this life in the most comfortable and least disruptive way possible, not stressing about small issues, but perhaps trying to secure a measure of fame. For the religious, the purpose in life should clearly be to do those things that will secure them a place in the better afterlife. In the case of escapable reincarnation, the logical purpose should be to seek a way out.

We can take the two situations that lead to specifics, and examine them in greater detail. First, the Dual or Multiple Afterlife situation assumes some rules that somehow prevent a person from joining the divine consciousness. There has to be a practical way to manage such rules. The coarsest way this might be managed is that a god simply enables people to attain the necessary level of consciousness if they have followed the rules he set forth, and demote their level of consciousness – such that they can only perceive another, less pleasant set of dimensions – if they have broken the rules. The problem with this coarse form is twofold. The most obvious is simply the question "where is this other less pleasant set of dimensions?" We have already found a possible place for heaven – in the set of dimensions that the universe might have been created in – but the other afterlives remain a mystery. The second objection is purely aesthetic. It seems unlikely that, considering the elegance evident in the observable universe, and in the laws of physics, that the creator would suddenly seem like an entity with direct influence over the universe rather than a subtle force, carefully present in all the universe's workings.

In other words, given the nature of the universe as it stands, the creator would have probably developed a natural process to determine which afterlife spirits would move on to. The problem with such a process is that some of the more specific requirements that religions impose on their followers simply cannot be accommodated. On the other hand, it is inconceivable that a deity with decent insight and an impressive understanding of time would actually use some of these criteria to determine which afterlife a soul will be sent to. So, if people are willing to accept that the deity has some irrational pet-peeves, then perhaps the possibility that the deity would build those into a natural selection process does not seem so absurd.

The most likely criterion that might be used to determine who reaches heaven, and who gets sent to hell, would probably be the state of a person's extra-body consciousness. If that consciousness is sufficiently aware, free of obsessive attachment to the physical world, and not plagued by guilt from actions in the world, which can cloud thought and therefore cloud the consciousness, then that soul can be brought up the rest of the way. This also leaves ample room for honest faith – since it is through faith in God and the afterlife that a person can become freed of attachments to the physical world. On the guilt issue, faith can cut both ways – if a person believes that God is angry about some action, then that person has more guilt than would be present without faith, but on the other hand if a person believes that God, with infinite compassion, will forgive their wrongdoing, then the guilt might be diminished. Taking a variety of religions into consideration, these elements explain the common ground between them. In fact, in a way, all religions could be mutually correct. The key to the specifics in religions is that they actually tell a person what to be guilty about. They could actually be self-fulfilling prophesies – if a person really believes the religion, they will experience guilt from the times they transgressed the specific tenets of the religion, and that guilt will cloud their consciousness and prevent them from reaching the more favorable afterlife.

The three criteria outlined above – improved consciousness, lack of guilt, and honest faith – might also be what the divine expects humanity to accomplish to escape a cycle of reincarnation. However, because in this case there is a greater amount of time allowed to human beings, it is reasonable to assume that the divine would expect us to go further, perhaps to attain some semblance of universal consciousness, or exhibit some weak communication with that plane of existence. There need not be any specifics, but the comments about guilt and being tied to this plane of existence probably also stand.

The simple fact that we cannot know what might occur beyond the scope of our lives limits us to a few basic conclusions. The rest is all a matter of faith. Those basic conclusions show, however, that there are very few possible purposes to life. And yet, despite the small range, people are still denied the ability to pursue the breadth of that range. This is the pursuit of happiness. Whatever might satisfy that pursuit without interfering with the happiness of others should be allowed to people, otherwise they cannot be considered free. That is the best measure of the balance between freedom and safety, but unfortunately it is not in the interest of those who have disproportionate power to promote that measure, since it would diminish their influence. The hierarchies of organized religion do not pose many problems except in this area, where they have an interest in suppressing the balance, and limiting freedom of choice. With such influential leaders, capable of dictating what actions are worthy of damnation, religions have gained disproportionate influence on spiritual thought, often in contrast to the intentions of the founders of the religions. Barring that, the previously mentioned issues with Case A1, and the occasional human sacrifice during ancient wartimes, spiritual thought and faith has led to very little that might be considered objectionable or destructive.

Life's Purpose in Light of Eternity

As noted in the examination of afterlives in the previous section, the basic purpose of life, without consideration of anything beyond this life, is to live the most comfortable life possible, to pursue happiness and flee pain. To ensure that one individual's pursuit does not interfere with another's, we create culture, law, and government – often in that order. The three types of inevitable afterlives – A1 through A3 – simply create a continuum that attributes minimum importance to the basic purpose of this life at one end, and ultimate importance at the other end. If ultimate importance is placed on the basic purpose of this life, then there is often an accompanying desire for fame as a form of immortality among those who are not satisfied with mere comfort, but wish to increase the happiness of others, thereby ensuring remembrance. In the case of multiple afterlives where actions in this life determine where you go, there is the added purpose in this life to ensure a favorable position in eternity, based on whatever a person's beliefs might be. If escapable reincarnation is the form of afterlife we have ahead of us, then the basic purpose of life is still intact, but colored with either an effort to build up what might be called good karma – good deeds that would bring the soul closer to salvation in each successive lifetime – or to attain higher levels of consciousness each lifetime. Reincarnation that a person could not escape would eliminate the importance of karma, leaving only the basic purpose of life. Taking each one of these in turn will give us a good indication of the problems of modern life, and the kinds of understanding that would be necessary to improve life.

At first glance, merely being comfortable seems to be a fairly poor purpose for our existence, devoid of deeper meaning and significance. It is the purpose every animal on Earth has, and denotes no special significance to human beings. Naturally, that is exactly why it is the basic purpose of life extrapolated from our existence in this universe – we can assume that all other creatures similarly existing also have this purpose. Before we seek higher purposes to distinguish ourselves from our fellow beings, perhaps we should assess how well we have fulfilled this most base and shallow reason behind life, and compare it to how well mere animals have done.

Only in the past three hundred years has the Western world acknowledged that the pursuit of happiness is a natural right, and countries lacking representative government, or those with oppressive norms, still fail to recognize as one. The current attempt to introduce representative government to the Middle East will have to deal with the absence of this right in the existing culture. Both through history and in the modern day, there have been religious restrictions, which highlight major points about freedom of religion. Often times, religions oppose the basic purpose in order to emphasize the requirements made upon people to reach the better afterlife. This sort of religious tendency, of course, defies human nature, and because it contradicts nature, religion tends to assume that human nature is more evil than good. And since religion has made what is good opposite to what is natural, this becomes a self-fulfilling prophecy. But, in the end, religion might be correct, so rather than dismiss it, it is only necessary to give people the freedom of religion to ensure that it is compatible with the pursuit of happiness. After all, given choice and eternal perspective, people will seek the way that will most likely lead to happiness for all time. It is only the limitation of a person's perspective that leads to pursuit of immediate happiness over lasting happiness, and that lack of perspective will be discussed at length in further sections.

Aside from religious restrictions on the pursuit of happiness, there is the individual's interaction with the political realm. When cultures and laws become widespread, governments are created to mediate between individuals, and to ensure that one man's pursuit of happiness does not cause another man pain, and that the nation's comfort as a whole is protected from outside interference. That is, at least, the ideal purpose of government in its relation to purpose of individual life. Human beings create communities of independent individuals unlike anything found in nature, and government has become a necessity, though as some of the political theorists of American independence called it, a necessary evil. However, when government fails in this simple duty of mediating between individuals, it becomes an intolerable evil. In the modern era with our quick communication and transportation, it is also natural that some level of organization above national governments mediates relations between the governments. After all, countries can cause pain to each other in the quest for their own happiness, just like individuals can. The key for an organization mediating relations between nations – the United Nations being the most important, but another is the highly contentious World Trade Organization – is that it respects the freedom of nations as if they were individuals.

Again, problems occur when this does not function in its ideal manner. It is fair to say that no government has been built to achieve this very basic function smoothly and with minimal transgressions against the freedoms of the people. The modern republic, with its representation and accountable decision-making bodies, is likely the best system history has seen, but while it is on the whole decent, it still produces its intolerable moments. Those moments rising out of the problems of party politics will be dealt with in the section on government, and those spawning from justice in that section. Aside from these specifics, it is the responsibility of the government to establish a baseline quality of life that the government itself should be responsible for. In other words, people contribute to a government to be protected from pain and to secure their freedoms, so the government has to decide what pains are within its capabilities to prevent against.

All governments are required to defend against foreign attack, so what we are really discussing is the domestic level. Should the government be responsible for safe drinking water, for health care, for providing food, for disaster compensation and repair, for getting care for those with psychological disorders, for building houses for the homeless, for finding jobs for the unemployed, or for taking care of the retired? A government's responsibilities should be proportional to what citizens contribute to that government. This should not be interpreted on the individual level – in other words, simply because the rich pay more taxes than the poor does not mean that they should receive from the government a higher base quality of life, since that would be redundant. The average taxes per capita should be the number taken into consideration, and the benefits should be evenly offered – with individuals choosing whether they require assistance in all but the cases of socially disruptive psychological disorders, in which case it is a matter of public safety. There are other services besides taxes that citizens are required by the government to provide, and these should be taken into account. Taxes are simply the easiest to calculate.

Some might respond, saying that programs like welfare might give people incentive to remain unemployed. If the general opinion of society is in agreement with this logic, then the government should not provide such a program, but as a result taxes collected by that government should be proportionally less than one that provides all services including welfare. If a government provides an incomparable base quality of life, then citizens under that government should be expected to contribute more money. Needless to say, this is not how government currently operates.

It can be argued that this would not be economically viable, but it does agree with the principle of the pursuit of happiness and government's role. Despite the fact that economics was originally meant to show how nations might better their welfare, and therefore their collective happiness, it has been one of the greatest offenders against the pursuit of happiness for the past thirty years. Adam Smith wrote *The Wealth of Nations* to encourage European countries to move away from the isolated economies fostered in mercantilism, and towards open trade which would not only benefit national economies, but also human welfare as a whole. Smith did not explicitly say so, but the interdependence true free trade implies also means that there is greater political stability. Since war causes serious disruptions in the flow of goods, people who can afford those goods, or require those goods, would be quick to oppose war. An underlying reason to keep government influence out of the economy – as in laissez-faire capitalism – might be to prevent the kind of economic manipulation that would lead to political strife.

The theories of capitalism were developed to combat the illogical system of mercantilism, which was creating strife – in the colonies that would become the United States, not to mention most of continental Europe. Capitalism was in full agreement with the pursuit of happiness. However, the modern business world, encouraged by relatively new theories about the way wealth is generated, has developed an edifice that is unsustainable. An example of the new theories is trickle-down economics, which proposes that government intervention to aid large businesses and to give the top earners tax breaks will eventually help everyone in the society. Alone, the idea is not entirely without merit, but combined with a business atmosphere that holds workers in contempt and layoffs as a way of keeping profits high, it does not have its intended affect.

This trend of attitudes and theories in the business world began in the 1970s, and a graph of real household wages since 1970 will show that it has noticeably flattened compared to decades before, despite the fact that households now frequently have two wage earners instead of one. Within the economic world there are competing theories – particularly theories that support the welfare state, healthcare, and other social systems – that would be more conducive to the pursuit of happiness. In general, when business practices are clearly getting insidious, there is a need for change in the operant theories in the system. Today, the way for companies to make money is usually centered on mergers and layoffs as a means of cutting costs and reducing competition, and advertising to entice young consumers who have not established brand loyalties yet. Tomorrow, perhaps businesses will only think to profit on innovation, and would be ashamed to be forced to layoff workers. For those who think that such a mindset would be impossible for business, the precedent is already etched in history – it was the prevailing attitude before the Great Depression. Until the 1929 stock market crash, an employee – from manufacturing to services – could expect to work with a company for decades, not be laid off after months.

Criticisms aside, it is clear that the human race has developed its ability to pursue happiness far beyond the ability of animals, even though our systems are far from perfect. Of course, the fact that our pursuit of happiness does not take the ideal form might be an indication that we should pay more attention on this life and how we live it. Until as a community we consider where we are headed, and examine thoroughly the future before us, the debate about what might be the best systems will be a matter of personal opinion. What is not a matter of opinion is the way we have dealt with the avoidance of pain.

In the twentieth century, the human race achieved levels of comfort unmatched in any century before, but also managed ways of blowing up that comfortable world scarcely imagined before. In fact, between the holocaust and the atomic bomb, the initial glowing view of our world a visitor from the past might have of modern life would take a severe hit, all the way down to cautious ambivalence. It is rare for creatures in the wild to kill for anything but food, and in disputes with another member of the same species, animals will often injure without killing. Only ants, aside from humans, wage what might be considered war. Human beings have developed a talent for causing pain to other members of the same species, and every increase in technology seems to lead to new casualty levels in warfare.

Here we have a project for ourselves in this life. So, as a purpose, seeking pleasure and avoiding pain without denying the right to others is still a goal we need to achieve. It is not beneath the consideration of human beings for the simple reason that we have not achieved it yet. Expanding the ability to seek pleasure can be taken gradually – though in nations with non-representative governments there might be more pressing need to consider this element. Avoiding pain, however, requires serious and immediate thought, followed by careful action, considering the bloodiness of the twentieth century and the unpleasant start to the twenty-first. As Voltaire has his main character say at the conclusion of *Candide*, after the optimistic view of what has happened is explained to him, "All that is very well, but let us cultivate our garden." We should not ignore flaws in our systems, believing that they are the best ones possible, and assume a fatalistic view of the future.

Nor should we turn away from the wisdom that has brought us so far, by turning the systems on their heads. By cultivating them, as Voltaire suggested, we will move along road and have good reason to be optimistic, and to look forward to rather than dread the future.

If it seems that simply seeking comfort in life provides no meaning to this life, and adds nothing to our experience, it should be considered a step, and not the entire journey. Once we have reduced the suffering in the world, we will be better able to decide what further goals to pursue. It is, on the other hand, difficult for someone starving in Africa to consider the grander questions of purpose in life. For a family in a nation torn by war, their only interaction with the divine might be for solace, and praying for peace. That family is not at all concerned about the theories I write about, or any abstract considerations. And in areas of peace and plenty, there is still unemployment, illness, and any number of other things that ensure that people are not free to give thought to higher understandings and other purposes. To some extent, these practical, every day problems lead people to systems of beliefs, including both religion and other spiritual systems that attract large numbers of people, because they simply do not have time to think about the divine, and do not have faith in their own abilities, and so rely on others to think for them.

But once we satisfy the basic purpose in life, we may conclude that some of the systems that involve afterlives are, in fact, useful to pursue. Some readers are, no doubt, fairly comfortable in this life, and feel themselves free to ponder the next life, so let us move onto those. The leap from matters confined to this life and culture to the possibilities of the next life and the divine, which is beyond time, is a dramatic – and, in fact, infinite – one.

Having already noted some of the pitfalls of religion, let us acknowledge some of its contributions. Religion makes

Purpose in Life

accessible to vast amounts of people a great scope of time, as events occurring thousands of years before are given immediate relevance. People feel that they have a connection to the past, even if that past is culturally different from the modern day. They have models to work from, figures to look up to, that neither the pursuit of comfort, nor honest historical inquiry can provide in such abundance. When faith is not entangled with culture, it can be the agent for determining what virtues are to the benefit or to the detriment of society. Belief in definite values provides a check against the tendencies of culture, which works on whims and the relatively short-term trends within the society. The connection to the past that religion – and anything that works on the level of eternal perspective – provides can help us to identify the more ephemeral trends in life, like the fads of consumer culture, and ignore them.

The purpose of life that religion represents is to do what is necessary to get to the better afterlife. In essence, it is to prove that one is worthy of entering heaven. Given that, religious institutions have a great deal of authority to wield – they can determine what will lead a person to heaven and what will lead to hell in those cases that are not already determined in sacred texts, extrapolating their judgments from the beliefs of the religion. The importance of the religious way of life, then, is the role its powerful central institutions (particularly whatever form of church and clergy the religion may have, but also the actual practices of the religion can also become influential institutions) play, and the response of believers to these central institutions.

Religion gives its authority both to ideas and to people, in a way no other form of spirituality can. While this power is somewhat diminished in the modern day, with the current dominance of consumer culture, it is still potent. This means that religion has an amazing responsibility to seek the truth in every matter, and analyze situations carefully without being inflexible to the changes time demands. Of course, religion rarely fulfills this responsibility, and often becomes irrelevant or subjected to the pressures of culture as a result. Religion should be structured philosophy, with its inconsistencies resolved rather than ignored. The fact of the matter is in sharp contrast to the ideal here, and because of the discrepancy, religions often fracture into smaller components. When Protestantism split from Catholicism, it was because inconsistencies were not being resolved, and men like Luther and Calvin decided to create resolutions that the church would not accept.

Ideally, religious authorities would also be careful about their opinions on matters, particularly about how those opinions are spread. Religions often seek to impose opinions not only on followers of the religion, but also on those who have chosen other ways. For some reason, religions tend to create extremist groups within their ranks, and when those groups gain authority, they create strife between belief systems. Fundamentalist and proselytizing groups come out of religion more than other types of belief system precisely because of the strong central institutions religion can create. The power given to those institutions is tempting, and people with strong convictions and a great deal of power rarely like others disagreeing with them. Religion is at its worst not when its opinions are wrong, but when its opinions are forced on those who follow other faiths. When opinions are wrong, only those who refuse to examine their opinions carefully are hurt. When opinions are forced on others, there is strife, and often death, on all sides.

Therefore, religion has great effect on the ways of this world, and that effect can be beneficial to the basic purpose of life and the higher purpose that the religion supports at the same time. It can broaden the understanding of time by giving events of long ago present importance. Slaves in the American South during the nineteenth century, for instance, associated their own desire for emancipation to the Exodus of Moses, the biblical story in which Moses freed the slaves in Egypt and brought them to the Promised Land. They used the story of the Exodus to give them hope, and help them to endure one of the most atrocious tragedies of the modern era. Religion gave them the bridge between themselves and events that occurred three thousand years before.

Religion also insists that the eternal and divine should be considered constantly. Ideally, this would result in people refining their understanding of the universe and its purpose, but religion alone cannot achieve this end. People must be educated, and must be capable of being intellectually involved with the religion, and not just emotionally involved. This is why, throughout the medieval age, the Christian church was so void of constructive understanding. The lack of education and intellectual involvement led the church fathers to rely on the knowledge of Aristotle before them, despite the fact that Aristotle was a pagan. Aristotle was relied on more than other thinkers, though others like Ptolemy the astronomer would be given a place in doctrine, because he created an immense body of work that looked like a complete philosophy, and he had not said much that would contradict Christian doctrine. The church argued that Aristotle could not have done such great work without God having intended for him to do so, and that Aristotle was meant to provide the knowledge base that would support Christianity, so the new religion would not have to develop knowledge on its own.

Hierarchy has an intrinsic interest in limiting education to the masses, and church hierarchy is no exception. At the end of the medieval age, though, the Jesuits, ardent defenders of the Catholic faith, did indeed establish academies and were well known for their emphasis on education. The Jesuits educated many of the finest thinkers of the Enlightenment and the Age of Reason, so it is clear that church hierarchy is capable of rethinking self-interest for the sake of society, when society has made clear its grievances in the way the Protestants had. And, of course, it must be remembered that a priest in the church – Copernicus – was the one to contradict the Ptolemaic Earth-centered model of the universe, and thus spark the entire scientific movement, so the limiting influence of religion should not be exaggerated.

For the effect of religion to reach its ideal, the religion's adherents must be intellectually involved, and dynamic in their ability to consider the questions of the universe on the basis of their beliefs. Traditionally, faith alone has been emphasized, but faith is understood to be an emotional attachment devoid of recourse to logic or deep thought. That leaves a person susceptible to intellectual confusion and the incompatibility of belief and knowledge. Without the ability to examine beliefs intellectually, the only step an individual trying to resolve such an incompatibility can take is to keep an extremely narrow perspective that ignores any evidence that might contradict faith. This defeats the eternal perspective, and keeps a person focused on the shorter time spans that culture operates on.

Intellectual involvement in one's beliefs is the only way a person can fully benefit from religion's ability to transcend culture. Otherwise, even if the church's hierarchy is careful in its dealings with culture, the average believer will be so tied to cultural norms that at best people will be limited by culture's short sense of time, and at worst there will be a struggle between culture and the church, which the culture will inevitably win unless the church uses force. This dynamic can be seen in early and medieval Christianity, at which time various deviations from the official Christian doctrine develop locally to conform to the local culture. At the very beginning, of course, Christian doctrine itself had to negotiate with local culture, as can be seen through its lack of acceptance in Israel, the travels of the proselytizers through other lands, and finally the impact made by Christians in Rome itself. Roman culture was notoriously tolerant, but because Christianity violated power relations within the society – introducing an alien form of equality that challenged the emperor's claim to power – Christians faced oppression until the negotiation between their spirituality and the established culture could take place. Once Christianity became established and set forth an official doctrine, local variations to accommodate culture would be called heresies and crushed. Often, the heresies rose not out of any malice to the central authority, but to accommodate a different world-view perpetuated through a strong local culture.

Culture can be right, of course. Having a narrow view and a narrow span of time to draw information from does not mean that the conclusions of that view are necessarily less correct. It only means that there is less information to base conclusions on, which is in some cases helpful. On more trivial matters, a narrow perspective reduces needless complications. A person who bothers considering the cosmic implications of buying a certain kind of shirt, for instance, would not get very far in life, and might as well have just bought whatever fit the current fashion trend. Also, the smaller perspective is also useful when decisions have to be made quickly – the human condition, after all, centers on the short amount of time we have on Earth. If culture was not helpful, it would not be looked to for answers. The problem with culture is that it can dominate life, since it operates on everyday affairs, but cannot be corrected in the gentle way individual experience can be, and is not lofty like history and religion are. Since there is a deeper discussion on perspective in the sections ahead, we can refrain from delving into the peculiarities of culture any further here.

Time and the Human Condition

Escapable reincarnation produces more extreme relationships with culture than a dualistic afterlife does. On the one hand, it can be totally subsumed by culture, while on the other it can be completely aloof of it. Since in this form of spirituality, people need not obey hierarchies – or, at least, they have many lifetimes to – there is no authority to keep the spirituality separate from the influence of culture. On the other hand, there is no authority to give culture divine justification.

Culture can completely absorb the spirituality, creating rituals and ceremonies that the original system has no logical connection to. The wild variations of Buddhism are a good example of this, with local cultures creating their own practices, and often their own set of divinities. At the other end of the spectrum is the ascetic, who removes himself from the culture and worldly possessions. In some cultures, it is considered the norm to support these ascetics, while in others they might be shunned, but in any case the figure is always a person who understands the incompatibility of the spiritual level of thought and material attachments – attachments supported by culture – and so chooses one over the other.

In general, the sort of continuum between these two extremes is impossible in orthodox religion (excluding heresies), since hierarchies eventually take over. The monastic orders were originally meant to be a way for believers to separate from society and pursue spiritual thought in Christianity, but instead the monasteries built hierarchies, acquired wealth, and were intimately involved with the struggles of the culture. Because of the immediacy of a persons fate in the religious case – case A4, which allows only one lifetime before divine judgment – hierarchies are simply a natural result, because there are only few people confident enough to make conclusions that might determine the fate of souls, while there are many in desperate need of guidance.

Purpose in Life

The purpose of life that the case of escapable reincarnation produces – to build up good karma or to attain higher consciousness – has the practical effect of encouraging people to resolve differences without resorting to culture, law, or government. This is mainly due to the reduced authority people are willing to give to those systems when there is no divine justification for them, and no immediate threat of damnation people must face for disobeying the institutions. Even when a society is not theocratic, the institutions of law and government in particular will employ spirituality in rituals and mottos. In the escapable reincarnation such invocations should have far less effect since there is no immediacy to the search for salvation.

To attain its ideal form, escapable reincarnation requires a society where there is an optimistic view of human nature, because then people will collectively attempt to govern themselves, with criminals being few and manageable. In more pessimistic societies, there is no expectation humans will strive to good karma and higher consciousness, and people will actually seek authority. This might have been what led to the original rise of the Brahmin caste in Hindu society, and the overlaying of a dualistic afterlife onto the escapable reincarnation at the heart of Hindu belief. According to Roman sources, the Celts in ancient Europe after 100 B.C. also believed in a form of reincarnation – whether it was escapable is uncertain – and it is possible that internal turmoil might have been one reason Christianity looked attractive, and Celts often readily converted.

The various goals that might be pursued in this life create structures around them, and the main purpose of these structures is to mediate between individual and individual and between individual and the divine. The pursuit of happiness and avoidance of pain is a deeper and more difficult purpose than it might seem at first glance, and must be adequately satisfied, if not ideally satisfied, before an individual can seriously consider greater purposes in light of what might be beyond this world. Looking to what might be beyond, there are only two commonly believed possibilities that substantially diverge from the basic purpose, and they are defined most by the time they allow for a person to satisfy the requirements to move on to the better plain of existence – religion gives one lifetime, while escapable reincarnation allows many.

This simple difference, however, is significant to the interaction between purpose in life and the dictates of culture. With religion, the interaction between spirituality and culture is mostly in the hands of the church hierarchy, and there are a range of possibilities from spirituality legitimizing the culture to spirituality and culture engaging in a struggle against each other. For those who believe in escapable reincarnation, the interaction is mostly in the hands of individuals, and it can range from culture totally dominating spirituality and its requirements to a spiritual man removing himself from the culture.

Purpose in Life

Cultivating the Human Garden – Legitimate Communities

As discussed in the previous section, the basic purpose of life is to simply cultivate the human garden, to produce a situation in which pleasure is to the greatest possible degree ensured, and pain is limited, so that individuals can finally rise above daily toil to better examine the universe, and consider what higher purposes should be pursued. It is important that the pleasure-pain part of the basic purpose is not taken to be the end purpose in life. It is necessary to fulfill the basic purpose, and challenging to do so, but critics of it would be right to say that there has to be more to life.

This can be compared to Maslow's hierarchy of needs, except that the pursuit of pleasure and protection from pain is at the lowest level instead of food, water, and shelter. We can call it a hierarchy of purpose instead, and it should only be compared to Maslow's hierarchy at the structural and conceptual level, and not in the specifics. While food, water, and shelter are necessary to pursue pleasure and reduce pain, they are far from all that is necessary, and while self-actualization, the highest need in Maslow's work, seems to be an admirable ultimate purpose, it is ill-defined and therefore useless. What are the higher levels in the hierarchy of purpose? We have very little indication of this, because so few people have gotten beyond the basic level. To find what might lie beyond, we must first get beyond the first level. Perhaps it would be adequate to ensure that the first level consumes only little of our thought or energy, instead of the bulk of it. To cultivate the human garden, then, we should ensure that the communities we have built to help us collectively fulfill the basic purpose actually fulfill that goal.

That communities were originally built for collective security is clear through history and anthropology, so protection from pain is acknowledged as the basis for community. The pursuit of pleasure comes in when the community makes unfair encroachments on individual freedoms – encroachments that cannot be justified on the basis of collective security. Power relations in a community are an attempt to negotiate between the protection from pain and the pursuit of pleasure. Only in the seventeenth century was it theorized that community should actively protect the pursuit of pleasure. Representation within the government would provide the individual with greater control and awareness of power relations, and therefore allow the people to find how best to prevent one person's pleasure from inducing pain on another, instead of leaving such decisions to an autocratic monarch who is only interested in his own pleasure.

The reason for this shift in the seventeenth and eighteenth century was a combination of political developments – absolutist monarchies in particular – and a new search for knowledge independent of biblical knowledge. The new search for knowledge started with basic principles, one of which was the principle of Natural Rights. The Stoics formulated Natural Rights long before the Enlightenment, but their work was forgotten through the Dark Ages. There are certain rights that no community, regardless of the need to protect from pain, can deny its citizens, because to deny those rights would go against the very nature of rational beings like humans. During the turbulent times when governments were actually enshrining these rights, Locke declared these to be life, liberty, and property, while Jefferson stated it in the Declaration of Independence as life, liberty, and the pursuit of happiness. Life is obvious – a person does not agree to join a community to attain a degree of safety only to be killed by the community itself. Liberty is general, but it implies that only the freedoms that might be detrimental to safety of the community should be limited, and all others should be reserved to the individual. Property is a subset of the pursuit of happiness. In the century between Locke and Jefferson, there was a discussion about whether property in particular was a natural right, and Jefferson's generalization was his way to resolve this dispute. While there might be some question whether property is a natural right, few who accept the idea of natural rights altogether will dispute that the pursuit of happiness is one of them. The considerations about Natural Rights and how to protect them emphasized the need for representative government, and ensured that such governments would be responsible not only for security, but also be actively aware of the pursuit of happiness. Modern governments are expected to provide a certain quality of life to its citizens. The idea of legitimate community that follows does not base its claims on the idea of Natural Rights, nor does it claim that nurturing communities are necessarily natural. However, the idea has been informed by the rights outlined, so a basic understanding of the concepts behind them can be useful.

    A community can be any group of people who live under a set of doctrines – either cultural, spiritual, or in law. So a city, with its own local government, can be considered a community, but it is beholden to the real level of authority – the national government. In this case, it will be clearer to confine the discussion to communities of the national level, though the ideas are technically applicable to any community. It follows from a community's reason for being that there are certain qualities any community must fulfill in order to be considered legitimate. Without these qualities, the community would not be working toward the basic purpose, and is in fact doing more harm than good to the individual.

Time and the Human Condition

In light of our discussion of purpose in life, the most essential qualities are freedom of belief, freedom of expression, equality before the law, time to pursue individual happiness, and sustainability, though political theorists have proposed other qualities that might be of significant importance. The first four are all under the natural right of liberty, while sustainability – the ability of a good community to perpetuate itself for future generations – is a concern that has developed since the mid-twentieth century, when we began to realize that we were capable of depleting our natural resources. If a community depletes its resources, then no matter how good it is in the other areas, the pleasure of the current generation comes at the cost of pain to future generations. As will be shown in the explanations that follow, the lack of these five essential qualities will result in one idea of how to pursue happiness interfering with pursuit of other ideas. These are central liberties that have to be present before a community can claim to be obeying the natural right of the pursuit of happiness. Because of their centrality, they can be used to distinguish a legitimate community – one that obeys the rights, needs, and purposes of its constituent individuals – from one that will inevitably limit people from overcoming the first level of the hierarchy of purpose, and hinder the ability to seek higher purposes.

Very few systems of spiritual belief actually demand persecution of those who disagree with the system's tenets, and in those it often requires specific interpretations of particular passages before such intolerance becomes divinely justified. In most cases, spiritual intolerance is more often a case of spirituality's entanglement with culture and cultural norms than a requirement established in the texts or teachings. Despite this natural tendency to toleration within spiritual systems themselves, intolerance is standard among religious cultures. In the modern world, however, the problem is mostly how to define freedom of belief than trying to convince people that it is a reasonable proposition, so the discussion that follows will examine how this freedom should be interpreted, and not try to advocate this necessity when it is already enshrined in so many constitutions.

Freedom of belief has to include all forms of belief, and not simply religion. If we try to discuss freedom of religion instead of freedom of belief, we risk allowing only a very confined form of spirituality, and the community can further allow restrictions on others by simply redefining 'religion.' And the term belief should not be limited to mean spiritual belief, since in that case the community can demand that people must belief in some form of spirituality. The meaning of this freedom should, in other words, be construed as broadly as possible.

But what does freedom of belief mean? If a person believes something, a government can hardly force him to believe something else, since short of a lie-detector test there would be no way to probe the beliefs of an individual. At face value, it seems to be a moot point. In fact, the community can attempt to determine the beliefs of an individual – through education, reinforcement, and limiting contact and communication to holders of deviant ideas. The beliefs of an individual can be at least confined to a narrow range by such attempts, if not totally determined by the society. An individual immigrating into a society may have a broad view of different beliefs, but that individual will have difficulty introducing that broad view to his or her children if the community uses education and other means to narrowly define belief. Education should always be an introduction to information, possibility, and perspectives, and never an inculcation of beliefs since children lack the ability to be critical of ideas, or to conclude whether certain beliefs will actually lead to their happiness. The separation of church and state is most vital because education is typically controlled by the state, and the government of a cultivating community should be careful that, within schools, no favoritism or explicit positive reinforcement is given to support a particular set of beliefs. That being said, schools should not be stifled by unreasonable regulations. Anything can be taken to a tyrannical extreme, so reactions should be carefully balanced to maintain individual freedom.

So even though belief is something private, residing in the individual's mind, a community has the ability to change belief, and the freedom of belief is designed to prevent this. This means, then, that even in the most progressive nations, we are still on the road to true freedom of belief, and there is likely still a long road ahead. While that is true, it is simply a reflection of the fact that we are not perfect. Using perspective we can see that, in those nations where the freedom of belief is in some way officially enshrined, we have come a long way from the attitudes of even a century ago. In the mid-nineteenth century, it would have been rare for a person to find a book accurately describing spiritual beliefs other than those subscribed to by his society, despite the fact that printing was already widespread and affordable. The transformative effect of the freedom of belief is nowhere more evident than in bookstores today, and its reach can be measured by the diversity of ideas presented by the books in those shops. In some areas, the freedom has not taken hold as absolutely, held back by cultural barriers, and the bookstores in those areas will reflect it. The internet can also be seen as a reflection of the wide range of ideas people are now open to, though it cannot reflect the geographic variations. We are, in other words, on the right road, and should not be overly concerned that we have not reached our destination. The key is to remember that we have not achieved the correct balance yet, that we still have improvements to make, and not to lapse into the complacent idea that we have reached the best state possible.

Purpose in Life

Aside for nations in which the government does not even pretend to be legitimate or attentive to the people, the freedom of belief should not be a major concern for us as we look to the problems in our communities. What about the freedom of expression? Expression includes speech, press, and action, and also stems from the discussion on purpose in life. Imagine, for instance, a situation in which the freedom of belief is guaranteed, but the freedom of expression is not. Clearly, the government would simply limit the ability of adherents of spiritualities power to express their faith in public, while saturating the media with the beliefs of those in power. Outside spirituality, there would also be the matter of culture. The government would limit the voices of cultural opposition and use law to defend the cultural norms established by those in power, and the dominant cultural ideas would be the only ones allowed in the public discourse. Freedom of expression is essential to the freedom of belief. Again, of course, all these freedoms have to be moderated by respect for the right of others to express their freedom, and issues of where to draw the line – where one person is infringing on another person's rights – represent the only time the government should intervene. That is why representative government is necessary – the collective will of the people should inform the government about where this delicate balance lies, so that the government acts on that knowledge, and not on the whims of the few.

Government should never claim to be the arbiter of values, and should be hesitant about acting when that role is thrust upon it. Because it acts on the freedoms in a more deliberate manner than culture does, representation and careful thought becomes absolutely necessary in government. Judging that the government was, in fact, incapable of such deep thought, the framers of the American Constitution prevented the government from taking any stand on freedom of speech, press, religion, or assembly, at all. As can be seen from current laws in the United States, the First Amendment has not functioned as an absolute bar, because the government has been expected to mediate on these issues. The framers were not at that early point aware of this, but any representative government will be required to mediate between the various parties in the society, and cannot avoid it without failing to govern. In the United States, of course, the problems were particularly acute because of the diversity inherent in the nation and the legacy of slavery. So, since there is no avoiding it, government should in the least be hesitant to involve itself in all but the most obnoxious cases of injustice.

In the world today, even though societies with representative governments also tend to have freedom of expression, the governments inevitably find ways to curtail the freedom in any way people will allow them to. It is far easier to govern a people that, though able to vote, are unable to criticize decisions when their representatives have made them. Those in the government might be completely convinced that the limitations on freedom are for the best causes, but ultimately the government will go too far. Power, in the hands of those with anything less than perfect perspective, corrupts. As will be discussed in the section on government, there is widespread use of fear as a tool to encourage people into thinking they need more protection from others than is actually necessary. It is an absolute rule that any limitation of the freedom of expression will disproportionately benefit the powerful. So, there is a natural tendency over time for the freedom to diminish when no attention is paid to it.

Another problem with the way the freedom of expression is managed is the fact that those with more money have incomparably greater ability to express themselves. While some might say that those who are wealthy deserve to use that money in any way they choose, the fact is that the forums allowed to those of limited means are virtually nonexistent, and people desperately want to be heard. There are literally millions of websites on the internet created by those that made use of free web hosting services to get their voice heard on the world wide web, so it is clear that the cost of communicating their ideas is the only limiting factor for some people. As an alternative media, the internet proposes a problem by its sheer volume – only well promoted and advertised sites will get the kind of attention the mainstream media expects. So, there is an imbalance in the forums of expression, and this imbalance, as all imbalances inevitably will, is to the benefit of the powerful. It is unlikely that this problem will be solved unless a new medium is developed, or perhaps an improved search engine designed to solve this problem on the internet alters that medium. The ultimate solution would require a reworking of the money-based incentive system. That system, however, is a keystone of modern society. It would be irrational to so drastically change the best system of community we have – not to mention one that allows unparalleled freedoms compared to anything seen before it – to only partially solve the limitations of freedom of expression.

Equality under the law should take little or no explanation, and barring some racial discrepancies it is well adhered to in societies with representative governments. It is necessary for the simple reason that people would not otherwise be able to defend their freedom of belief or freedom of expression – they would simply be thrown in prison on false charges when they tried to exercise their freedoms. There are many issues that complicate equality under the law – not the least of which is the role of money in law and the already mentioned issue of racism – but even more so than freedom of belief, equality under the law has improved dramatically. Compared to the kind of corruption that could be expected even in the early twentieth century, and the kind of vicious racism that dominated through the age of imperialism, immigration restrictions, segregation, and the American Civil Rights movement right up to 1964, we can be satisfied that the level of justice in the Western world does not require a complete rethinking of the system. Instead, preventing any regressions and maintaining efforts to more finely tune the balances of justice will satisfy the requirements of community. In the United States, regressions are prevented by the laws that came out of the Civil Rights movement, along with the Supreme Court cases that reinforced equality under the law. If those laws are repealed or not enforced, or were not more finely tuned by further court cases, then the community of the United States would be in violation of equality under the law.

In the three areas so far examined, there are massive differences in the degree to which certain nations guarantee the freedoms and equality. Criticisms have so far been based on the Western world, or more broadly, nations with representative governments, because these tend to have comparable systems with a narrow range of variation, at least in terms of these rights. For nations under monarchies, military dictatorships, or other non-representative governments, there cannot be any expectation that the general population will be given freedoms of any kind, because the limitation of freedoms always supports those in power, and non-representative governments need all the power they can get to stay in control. If such a government actually gives its people freedom, it is a pleasant surprise, but there should be no expectation that those freedoms will remain if the government finds them risky to its power.

A non-representative government is a sign of illegitimate community. It is conceivable that everyone in the community, at its founding, agreed to have a monarchy or dictatorship take the lead, and in that case the community is legitimate for that generation, because they made the collective decision that the non-representative system would serve them best. After that first generation, though, it is unlikely that the government will obey the population's opinions again, so the situation only guarantees pleasure for the monarch or dictator, and everyone else can only hope that the leader's pleasure coincides with their own. Such a system can barely satisfy the common understanding of the word 'community' at all, much less qualify to be legitimate in terms of guaranteeing pleasure and reducing pain for individuals other than the monarch. Again, if it manages to fulfill the requirements, it is by coincidence rather than design, and will therefore not satisfy sustainability. Perhaps an enlightened monarch might come along whose pleasure would be the pleasure of the masses, but his mindset itself is coincidence – not inherent in the design of the system – so that his predecessor and successor will likely have different ideas.

In addition to a representative government, there also needs to be a culture that values and maintains the freedoms and rights. It is futile to expect such freedoms to function properly in a culture that will strike down any value they have with restrictive norms. In such a culture, creating a stable and legitimate community will take time. Opening up education – ensuring that the education system is not used to inculcate restrictive cultural norms – will be essential, but also create an immense amount of discontent that ensures the project has to be undertaken internally by members of the culture itself, not by those perceived to be on the outside.

A less commonly discussed facet of nurturing communities is that they leave as much time as possible for individuals to pursue their own personal view of happiness. It is rarely enshrined in anything more significant than labor laws – in which the workweek might be limited to forty hours, and a certain amount of vacation time is designated. While it might be argued that people at work are seeking the funds which they believe will lead to their happiness, and therefore that time should not be counted against the community, such an argument is deceptive on a number of points. First of all, the average worker does not get paid a hundred percent of the value of his or her work – in fact, in manufacturing work most individuals receive a pitiful percentage of the value they produce. So, the majority of work is clearly to the benefit of others. Secondly, almost all of the average worker's salary will be used to pay for a home, food, water, and modern necessities like electricity and gas. These are not elements of a personal view of happiness, but rather what we all recognize as necessities. Finally, the kind of material pleasure money can buy is not what many people would seek, if given that time to pursue happiness. So, labor laws are essential to any industrialized community.

Insofar as nations have labor laws, they have so far been sufficient, though not ideal. The standard measure of time taken by the community is simply the average number of hours per year worked by individuals in a nation, with the modern upper limit usually set at two thousand hours, and among nations that keep the statistic, only the United States and Japan approach that number. The European countries in general give their populations far more time, including at least six weeks of paid vacation. All of this is far improved from the kind of work time expected from productive workers (as opposed to management or service workers) at the start of the twentieth century.

There is one major mitigating circumstance, however. At the start of the twentieth century, despite the fact that many women and even children were forced to work for pitiful wages, they composed a far smaller percentage of the working population than they do today. Starting in the 1970s, the workforce boomed with a massive influx of women, changing the structure of the family. Despite the fact that many households now have two wage earners instead of one, economic figures in the United States show that average real household income has increased only mildly since 1970. This means that, by household, far more work hours are being contributed to the community for only slightly more money than had been made by half those hours thirty years ago. Even though improvements have been made when considering changes over a century, the trend over the past generation has been in the wrong direction, at least in the United States. In a society with such vast resources and wealth, it should not cause any difficulties to the economy if greater effort was taken to give people more time for their own benefit.

Part of the reason for this unfortunate trend over the past generation is actually related to the greatest problem modern communities face today, namely the sustainability of the benefits of community. The reason for sustainability's necessity is simple – just as the community must ensure that the pleasure of one individual does not cause pain to another, it must also ensure that individuals in the future do not have to bear pain for the pleasure of people today. It is the same principle, simply stretched over time, over generations. And the principle does not operate simply a few generations into the future, but for all time. If we have reason to believe a system will eventually break down, we need to consider how to solve this problem. Problems that will arise within a generation are naturally more vital, and need to be focused on with more attention, but looking deep into the natural consequences of our systems centuries or millennia from now will benefit us today in indirect ways – by giving us greater confidence in our abilities, our communities, and our perspectives.

How far should this go? Well, we know for certain that in about four to five billion years from now the Earth will no longer be habitable due to the death of the Sun, so logically, for the sake of our global community, increasing our capabilities in the area of space flight is constructive and a worthy pursuit. In other words, we should practice considering everything, and to prioritize accordingly. Needless to say, if pollution makes Earth uninhabitable in a few centuries, efforts to remedy that problem should take precedent over establishing colonies on new worlds outside our solar system.

The difficulty with establishing a community that is sustainable even for the short period of a century is the simple fact of the short human lifespan. As discussed in relation to time, and will be discussed in terms of perspective, the time before and after an individual's life seems completely unreal, just as the individual's personal past and future, although a much smaller timeframe, seems like a dream. It is natural, therefore, that the generation in power will only think to maintain sustainability for as long as they are expected to live. This is not out of malice or stupidity, but rather because consciousness is limited to such boundaries at birth. In fact, what needs to be dealt with first and foremost, and what will be relatively easy to deal with considering the nature of human consciousness, are those areas that may be unsustainable in the very short term – that is, within a generation.

Oil consumption comes immediately to mind – the dependence on this resource by the world as a whole is an imminent problem and will doubtless cause drastic crises within the foreseeable future. There are many optimistic estimates about the remaining oil around the world, but estimates that claim that there is over a century of oil left fail to take into consideration inaccessibility and increased usage by newly industrialized nations. Long before oil actually runs out, it will become too expensive for the average person to afford. Even if we manage to make affordable cars independent of gasoline, there is still air travel to consider, not to mention shipping. Theoretically, this will be an issue for the present generations, and even under the limitations of perspective, people should be actively concerned about it. Instead, it is forcibly kept out of the public discourse, or clouded by discussions about the dependence on foreign oil which is the surface of the problem rather than the heart, and communities around the world are failing the test of sustainability at this easy to grasp level.

The real test of a community's sustainability has to be its forethought for times beyond a single lifetime. While this is certainly hard, it is clearly possible for the human consciousness to take in new levels of perspective, take the broader view into account, and to make decisions that would stand for centuries. Take the political theorists that established the republic of the United States, for example. In a single effort they created a system that has stood for over two centuries, and shows no signs of weakening. They had disputes on many points, but the arguments set forth in those disputes showed a clear understanding of the consequences of every decision far beyond the length of their framer's lives. The men who built the government of the United States had a clear idea from the start that they had the responsibility of creating a sustainable community above all other considerations. The one major flaw in their plan was on the matter of slavery, but even on that issue, which was kept out of serious discourse by the representatives from the South, there were already clear arguments noting that the institution was inimical to the ideals of a free society, and would therefore eventually be to the detriment of that society's values.

There is every reason to consider the future beyond our own lives, and reasonable forethought can be expected to produce excellent results for any society that has actively employed it. Even if sustainability is not explicitly enshrined in legal documents and founding doctrines, it is implicitly always the case that the founders of a community intended for the system to remain legitimate beyond their own lifetimes.

They would also expect their descendents to have the combination of flexibility and adherence to basic values that would ensure the community continued to fulfill its essential function – to increase pleasure and reduce pain for all individuals.

To best cultivate the human garden and construct nurturing communities, the least we should work toward is freedom of belief, freedom of expression, equality under the law, time to pursue personal forms of happiness, and sustainability. It should be the function of any government that claims to act in the best interest of its people to keep these elements in mind. As always, when trying to manage something constructive, it becomes valuable to maintain an optimistic view of human nature and other individuals. Nothing can undermine happiness within a community like mutual distrust, and often individuals within a community will abandon one of the freedoms or goals outlined above simply because they fear what something like freedom of expression might create in the hands of others, or what sacrifices they might have to make for sustainability, or a murderer going free because the law puts the burden of proof on the prosecution. Fear and distrust nullifies any community. Eventually all cohesion breaks down, allowing oligarchies, monarchies, or even dictators to arise. The most extreme example is clearly Nazi Germany, when Hitler played on the fear and distrust of most Germans against Jews, Communists, and other fringe groups, and used that to turn the Weimar Republic into his dictatorship. In this example, the fear and distrust that existed among the Germans was the product of the loss of the First World War, economic distress, and a general pessimism that prevailed in that country. So, as a prerequisite for positive change in any society, there has to be preceding optimism, or the allowance for change will be turned to destructive purposes.

Part 3
Perspective

Time and the Human Condition

On Possibilities

Our universe contains billions of galaxies and those galaxies in turn contain billions of stars. Around one of those stars is a planet, one of nine, which in turn has millions of species, one of which has a population of billions of individuals, each of which is composed of a number of atoms that should only be written in exponential form. All the components of the universe are constantly interacting.

Now consider chess. On a chessboard, there are sixty-four squares, thirty-two of which contain pieces. There are twenty possibilities for the first move by white – each of the either pawns may move either one or two squares forward, or each of the two knights may jump to either of two open squares. After those twenty, the possibilities branch out first to billions, then to further powers of ten, so that even a supercomputer can have trouble computing the values of the various possibilities.

However, the supercomputer can do a fairly good job of it, and so can we humans without algorithms that simplify the issue into mathematics. We are capable of, at any given time, analyzing a wide range of possibilities. Of course, the possibilities generated by thirty-two pieces moving on a chessboard are like nothing compared to the possibilities of the universe, but that only means that we must broaden our abilities to consider the greater problems of life with the same level of thought some people can put into a chess match.

How absurd is it, then, that we satisfy ourselves with oversimplifying major issues into two sides? When even in the first move of chess, there are twenty possibilities, why is it we only look at two possibilities, or similarly few options, in politics, economics, spirituality, and culture? Some might say that, with all the things an average human being has to worry about, there is some need for simplification in some areas. After all, rather than playing a single chess match, the normal human is often playing the equivalent of over a dozen simultaneous matches on even a calm day in life. The first objection to this is that there needs to be appropriate priority given to those matters that affect a large number of people. In a society that gives people the right to vote, a person has a responsibility to his or her fellow citizens to make an educated choice, but making an educated choice is impossible when there are only two, three, or even four options.

Consider chess again. Suppose we only programmed a supercomputer with the two most popular openings, and only two variations at each stage after the opening, and everyone who played the computer knew that this was the case. The computer would be beaten in the opening even by low level amateurs. The same would be true if three or four openings and variations were programmed. All the benefits of having a powerful processor and excellent memory would be completely undermined by the limitations of the programming. Similarly, with most people being of sufficient ability to decide between many possibilities in life, limiting the number of choices in any situation can only limit the exercise of that ability and limit individual freedom.

The second objection to the argument in favor of simplification is that, over time, people will become intellectually lazy. If in every important situation people are only given two choices, then eventually in every situation, they will only seek two choices. People will be unable to handle situations where they are given a large number of options and are asked to evaluate their relative merits. Currently, people are conditioned to expect oversimplification in public life and those things that affect a great number of people, while dealing with complication in private life, where there are constant hassles and decisions to be made that distract a person from being able to deeply consider anything else. While individual freedom should always be emphasized, people confuse distracting choices with freedom. It is actually detrimental to the welfare of the individual when people spend more time deciding what sofa to buy than how to vote on a particular issue or candidate. That minor decisions should take on such bloated importance in the modern era of haste is quite unusual and unexpected, but suggests that there is, indeed, plenty of time for people to consider more possibilities at greater length.

Perspective, in any stretch of time, requires an open field of possibilities, and only with a wide range can we apply our knowledge and decide which is best. If there are few possibilities, there is no point to having a broad understanding of the issue, because the conclusions derived from that understanding will most often not be represented. So, while in the section ahead perspective will be analyzed in the way it is affected by time, the actual basic limitation on perspective is what options a person has. If an environment offers only one option to a person – for instance, in spirituality, since it is in that area where such strict limitation is most often enforced – then it is hardly worth the person's time to broaden his or her perspective in that area. As will be seen in further sections, though, there are many powerful cultural elements which operate underneath the surface that can actually determine what possibilities are offered to a person, among which are the ways ideas are communicated to individuals, and the struggle between the attraction of novelty and the defense of tradition that underlies every culture. It is through sometimes subtle maneuvering that culture determines what possibilities a person is exposed to, and therefore in what areas a person might have a broader or narrower perspective.

Perspective

Time and Perspective

The examination of time is important to the average person for two reasons. Firstly, we are aware that our lives are fairly short, so we speculate about what might have come before, what might come after our lives, and what the purpose of life is. Secondly, events in the past and plans for the future affect us today. The first common reason to ponder time is usually considered the domain of spirituality and philosophy, while how the past and the future affect the present is examined by every individual constantly. When people plan tasks to do in a day, eat at a certain time even though they might not be hungry, and in fact whenever a person looks at a clock, there is a brief, narrow examination of time and how it might affect the present.

The problem in the modern day is how narrow this examination has become. There is a lack of perspective – with people so occupied with day-to-day matters it is difficult for them to take the time to see the long-term affects of anything. Of course, consumer economies are based on this flaw, offering credit to encourage people to buy things they don't need and can't afford at the expense of future prosperity. Politics is also influenced by this focus on immediate concerns, as people are unable to develop the far-reaching sense of time that is required to judge what the best policies are. Personal relationships are also affected, since there ends up being an over-emphasis on immediate pleasure, and an absurd inability to show patience through the tough times in relationships.

Perspective typically requires an examination of time beyond our own lives and limited experiences. Four levels of perspective can be delineated, and only the first one is dependant solely on individual experience. This first level is not insignificant. Most people are able to derive some perspective through interaction with others, particularly family members, by sharing experiences, lessons learned, and purely by the interaction itself. This is normally the heart of one's environment. It should not be confused with "nurture" in the old nature versus nurture debate, since that psychological issue deals with underlying issues, while perspective is by this definition a conscious assimilation of information. Rather, this first level is a person's social life. It allows a person to draw conclusions that will not be wildly alien to those around him, since the tools they use to build their perspective will be roughly similar to his own.

The next level up is the cultural level. Whereas the first level is limited by those who are alive at the same time as the individual, a few generations older or younger, culture can retain elements from centuries past. Culture gives us perspective through tradition, custom, and a kind of collective memory. The elements of individual identity that culture provide outline certain perspectives for a person, which they either accept or rebel against, but which are the established basis of discussion. For instance, there are certain things in American culture that have become established issues – abortion, gun control, gay rights, and other topics that inspire similar intensity – that the prevailing culture has outlined as being of importance. Except for established cultural agreement, there is no reason why these topics should take precedence over other issues, like drunk driving, the divorce rate, or poverty, which in some cases have been given attention before. The change in discussion topics currently occurs about every decade, but used to be far less frequent.

Since culture has defined the topics that need to be discussed, perspectives will naturally be more concentrated on those topics while being more vague on others, which are not being given attention. It is within the realm of culture to define the boundaries of perception by establishing norms, but it is also common for the fringe elements in society – who had little part in establishing these norms – to rebel against those boundaries and overcome artificial limitations. When Galileo turned his telescope to the sky, he was in the midst of such a rebellion, since the cultural norms of his day – established through the power of the Catholic church – discouraged questioning the existing view of the cosmos. The African-American population in the midst of segregation naturally opposed the perspectives imposed by the dominant culture of the American South, since it was utterly focused on maintaining their oppression and servitude. Those are basically the two reasons why people attempt to transcend the scope outlined by culture – because the narrow scope has blinded the culture to the truth, or because one result of the limited perspective is to cause individuals pain. Such rebellions usually involve an appeal to higher levels of perspective, and become important in the study of history.

Culture provides the guidelines that have been established by a society over time with the purpose to explain how best to live life, but such norms are always developed by the powerful, whether they are a majority or a minority. It synthesizes a much greater range of information, through time and space, than a person's personal relationships and interactions can provide, at the cost of being impersonal and promoting obedience rather than thought. Still, any sufficiently large group of people will naturally develop a culture of some sort, so it is an inevitable presence. Most perspectives gained through television, grade school education, popular fiction, and other mass outlets will cater to culture simply because it would be impossible to organize them in any other way. Their popularity and reach would be limited otherwise. There must be more than just a common language for communication. Cultural touchstones are necessary for the media to be affective.

The third level in perspective is historical when dealing with the past, and speculation in the future. In terms of time, this level deals with ideas that are so far in the past, or so far in the future, that analysis is required to connect it with the common day. Unlike culture, history's effects on daily life are not readily apparent. It takes some explaining to connect Henry Ford's mass production of cars to lawn mowing, but there is nevertheless a clear connection. Just as an example, as the automobile became more popular in the 1920s, this allowed suburbs to grow because people with cars were able to live further away from work. Before the 1920s, suburbs were simply nonexistent. Before the suburbs, of course, only the rich could afford their own houses with lawns (as opposed to crop fields), but the rich could also afford servants to tend the lawn. Only with suburbs could there be a situation in which the owner of the home would mow his or her own lawn, and therefore cars are necessary to the development of lawn mowing. That is a trivial example of historical perspective, yet it shows how history can examine the relations between disparate elements in ways that give greater understanding.

Where historical perspective is most important is when citizens are called to vote on issues, or for candidates in an election. Often, culture has an unfortunately heavy impact in these rare occasions when the population is actually given a voice. I say unfortunately because, as already noted, cultural codes are formed by those dominant in society. Even if people are not in the dominant group, and do not share the interests of that group, the prevailing culture compels them to vote in a way that will simply reinforce the existing powers. The historical and futuristic perspectives are typically critical and often ignored. Through history, for instance, a voter can tap into a wealth of political theory to make an informed decision. Examining the future, a person can look into environmental issues even though those issues are not in cultural discourse, and environmentalists are often ridiculed in that discourse. While culture can have backward looking scope of centuries and a forward looking scope of a generation, history has a scope of millennia and, for the future, estimates can be made for things like population growth, resource consumption, and economic development a century in advance based on historical knowledge.

The problem with historical knowledge is the way it requires analysis before its connection to the present day can be seen. The two narrower scopes, of individual experience and of culture, are ever-present and require no efforts or tools to understand. This means that, while historical perspective is necessary to manage the wilder excesses of culture, and the manipulations of those already powerful in a society, it is not readily accessible to the bulk of the population. As already noted, grade school education is centered on the cultural level, and even in high school history classes, the focus is instilling a particular interpretation of history that conforms to the views of the teacher, who is in a position of power, moderated by the dominant culture, which is represented by the teacher's superiors in the education system. The purpose is not to encourage the student to develop a unique understanding of history, and interpret the events of the past in such a way that might result in an interpretation substantially different from that of the teacher, or society in general. That sort of historical inquiry is confined to college, and perhaps even there only for upper division and graduate classes taken predominantly by history majors. While it is possible that a grade school student, on his or her own merits, develops some historical perspective, it is uncommon and is not the current purpose of education.

Because of this limited accessibility, the historical level of perspective is the least commonly utilized.

The fourth and broadest level of perspective available to any being within the universe is the eternal level, stretching from the beginning of time to the end of time, going far beyond the extent of recorded, or even archaeological, history. The areas that use this level of perspective include, but are not limited to, physics, spirituality, mythology, and geology.

Physics has already been discussed, and we have seen how it requires an understanding of time that goes far beyond history, and examines the beginnings of the universe. There are also theories on the state of the universe and what end it might have – either it continues to expand indefinitely, reaches a stable state, or falls back into itself. Similarly, geology can examine the Earth and life of the past, and predict how the Earth might change in the future.

Spirituality considers the creation of the universe, the reason for the creation, and occasionally looks at how the universe might end. All spirituality stretches to a time before things became the way they are now – before historical time. This time is mythological time, and while there are many myths that are not spiritual, almost all spiritual systems will include stories of this time. It should be noted that in this context, the word 'myth' should not be taken to mean 'stuff we no longer believe,' but rather refers to stories of times long past, before the human race entered into its current state. What occurs in the Bible before Adam and Eve are expelled from Eden is in mythological time because before that point, things were not as they are now. All stories of a Golden Age fall into mythological time, because the whole point of those stories is that we are not in a Golden Age now. They are meant to show a time before we entered into our current troubles, and perhaps suggest how to get out of those troubles. Utopias are in the mythological time of the future, because they propose times where things will be substantially different from the way they are now. The Iliad, then, is an epic legend for the Greeks, but also has a foothold in mythology. Many epics, including the Indian Ramayana, are a bridge between the age of mythology and the age of legend. Meanwhile, tales of the Titans, Zeus' rebellion, and Prometheus bringing fire down to mankind, were all clearly mythological to the Greeks.

The problems of this level of perspective are mostly particular to the way the perspective is employed. In all cases, very few people are allowed to develop their own interpretations using this level of perspective. In physics and the other sciences, it takes a genius – or at least someone deserving of a Nobel prize – to wield the perspective legitimately. In spirituality, it takes a prophet, avatar, or deity. In the rest of mythology, it takes a bard. Other individuals simply cannot convince many people if they come up with a new view of things in any of these areas, and can only apply existing knowledge after careful consideration equal or beyond that which historians apply.

The problem of physics and the sciences is that they are, like history, mostly inaccessible to the public. Unlike history, though, the sciences are not immediately necessary for anything in life, from everyday actions to political considerations. It should be noted that people often confuse science with technology. Technology is simply a result of science, and while it is important to everyday life, it can only be a vehicle for perspective. Technology offers no perspective or understanding, being only a tool, while science is very clearly a search for and propagation of understanding. So, a person primarily accesses the scientific level of the eternal level of perspective for personal development and understanding, and rarely for everyday concerns – the exception being for medical reasons.

Spirituality and mythology, on the other hand, have trouble in their relationship to culture. Spirituality has long been considered indispensable in daily life precisely because it served to explain the unexplainable. Long before measurements could be taken of various phenomena, people have asked why certain things are true. Sometimes spiritual explanations have been remarkably close to the truth, while other times it provides only blind guesses to explain the cosmos. In any case, it has always been dispensable, because without it, only philosophy has proposed any purpose to life. Like the sciences, which are actually a development out of one philosophical school, the grand body of philosophical knowledge is too obscure to be readily applicable in all but a few areas. Incidentally, philosophy works at all levels of perception, so that each philosophical school would have to be examined independently before they could be arranged in their most dominant perspective level. Spirituality provides clear prescriptions for people to follow, and is both readily applicable and in widespread use.

This regular interaction with the entire population means that spirituality is in constant communication with culture. But, as already explained, those with power can manipulate culture, leaving the less powerful to either follow or create subcultures and countercultures. If spiritual propositions contradict the aims of the dominant culture, the subcultures and countercultures will be given a reason to rebel. So, the dominant culture naturally seeks to mold spirituality so that it conforms, and social strife is avoided. Spiritual systems have not been aware enough of this cultural manipulation, and through time such systems loose focus on the grander level of perspective, and are brought down to reinforce cultural norms and goals.

On the other hand, spiritual systems in which there is an awareness of the affects of culture often take the wrong course

Perspective

– attempting in its turn to change culture. This, of course, means that culture is still allowed to determine the topics of discourse and debate, and still limits the perspective of spirituality to more mundane matters. This is not to say that issues at the forefront of culture are unimportant, but that they involve a far narrower perspective than spirituality is typically concerned with. However, without the interference of culture, spirituality would probably resemble the constant search of science and philosophy for ever greater knowledge of the universe and of the purpose of life. It would not be a solid, infallible edifice which is sometimes correct, but often unable to accept rational explanations simply because such explanations would undermine the authority of the powerful.

It is important to note that only a wider perspective can be used to judge the conclusions derived from each of these scopes. To contradict the assumptions of culture, individual experience can only result in a personal rebellion, but recourse to historical or eternal perspective will be convincing in general. In the following sections, aspects of culture will be examined with a historical perspective.

The first section will look at the shift from culture perpetuated through oral tradition to culture passed down through written tradition, how this was sparked in Europe by a shift in spiritual understanding, and how it has in turn affected our ability to grasp pre-Christian spiritual beliefs. This is a cultural issue because it is a matter of media, and also because while spiritual beliefs themselves require an eternal perspective, the way those beliefs are passed down are generational, and are limited by practical considerations. In fact, language itself is such a consideration. The language we use often limits the eternal perspective, and ideas beyond the level of culture often require entirely new sets of vocabulary. The second section deals with a much more fundamental, and presently important issue – the struggle between the new and the old within any culture, and the way this struggle in turn spills onto spirituality, science, and the understanding of eternity. The final section deals with how individual experience and culture operate on a single generation's politics and world view – in this case, the World War II generation – and shows why the broader perspectives have become increasingly necessary.

Perspective

Oral Tradition versus Written Tradition

Over time, the way information is passed from generation to generation, and from teacher to student, has changed. This in turn has affected our perception of time and our perspectives of the past. Ancient cultures passed on their most important information orally, with the master in the presence of the student. Modern culture and spirituality centers on the written word, which at first sight seems more solid and permanent, but also robs people of the need to memorize vast amount of information and make connections with it. The pitfalls of the lack of a balanced approach to learning creates a bias in favor of more recent culture and knowledge, since the great majority of written work was produced in the twentieth century. Even if oral tradition continues to be passed down, it is no longer taken as seriously as the written word. The gulf between the two ways of learning also has its impact on those who are interested in ancient spirituality, since the way information is taken in changes the way it is understood.

Though it is certainly debatable, the Vedas are likely the greatest achievement in oral tradition surviving, primarily because they prove that the ancient form of learning can accurately preserve a complex body of work. The Vedas are collections of verses that, in India, have formed the basis for spiritual discussion for since at least 1500 B.C., and have been passed down through the ages through oral tradition. Certain families in India were originally tasked to the keeping of the epic, and their family names indicated this. Other discourses,

Time and the Human Condition

often more philosophical like the Upanishads, followed the Vedas as a commentary on them, and it was through these that Indian spirituality first got its complexity. Epics like the Indian *Mahabharata*, the Greek *Iliad*, and the Irish *Táin* represent a different form of oral tradition that attempts to bridge spirituality and culture instead of focusing solely on spirituality, and so were intentionally changed to suit context as they were retold. The Vedas, like any document with central importance to spirituality, had to retain their form exactly, and successfully survived the millennia because they continued to be relevant. To this day, the oral tradition of the Vedas continues, showing us that whatever the claims of written tradition are, the ancient way can be just as permanent and accurate.

The problem is that once something is no longer relevant, it is forgotten. Of course, books can be lost in the same way as the material they were written on disintegrates, but the effect is not so absolutely immediate. Those who study the ancient world will face the trouble of lost oral traditions constantly. It may seem like some civilizations simply did not have epics or complex philosophies, but the fact of the matter is that they probably had ideas that would put most modern storytellers and religions to shame. These have simply been lost to time. But this was not necessarily due to writing. Rather, the ancient civilizations were not interested in spreading their knowledge or to proselytize others. If by some cataclysm all members of their society died, then the knowledge simply had no purpose. As long as their people continued, the knowledge would remain.

Certainly, even in civilizations where writing is more favored, teachers have always taught orally. Whether it was Buddha, Confucius, Socrates, or Christ, their students were the ones to write, often because they disagreed with another student's remembrances of the master's words. And of course,

Perspective

if Plato had not recorded (and sometimes embellished) the words of Socrates, think what it would do to our understanding of Greek Philosophy. Much would have been lost if students remembered rather than wrote ideas down, but then again consider how many books have been lost in the burnings of countless libraries, and ultimately the loss might be equal either way.

There is a standing question about why some civilizations had more interest in writing than others. The standard explanation for the Greeks is that the alphabet simply made writing easier to learn, and therefore made the written medium efficient. This explanation cannot even remotely be applied to the complex script of the Chinese, though, yet their written work is as or more extensive. In the case of the Chinese, wars between kingdoms might have demanded claims to legitimacy, which the copious histories and records would have provided. Chinese writing is also quite an art, perhaps increasing its popularity. In general, very particular circumstances determined the popularity of writing among some civilizations, not any superiority that they naturally claimed for themselves. Indians eventually chose to write their epics down shortly after the arrival of Alexander the Great, which made clear that their ancient spirituality might actually be threatened by the invasion of what they would have considered barbarians. Every culture believes its own ways are best. Modern writing-based societies have grafted their own values onto history, immediately seeing advancement where writing was and backwardness where it was not.

The emphasis on writing in Europe was primarily a Christian invention. More than the Greeks or early Romans, the Christians made writing important to European spirituality by first proselytizing broadly, then creating a doctrine and canon that would be kept in a great book. They were the first to keep their beliefs in a book, giving that form of tradition a sacred quality it lacked before. Until Christianity, writing had simply been record keeping, even if it recorded a great epic. From the adoption of Christianity as the official religion of the Romans in the fourth century A.D., the book was read in Latin, not in the native tongue, and it was endowed with even more mystery and divinity since it was accessible to only a select few. Latin was a relatively uncommon language, the common tongue of Europe at the time being Greek – the language the bible was originally written and read in. The reason for the reading of the Bible in Latin is clear – Europe was filled with oral tradition, and if the holy book was read in either the native tongue or Greek, it would be memorized. The power and mystic quality of the priesthood would be lost. Ultimately, if the early church had truly wanted to spread the word of God as far and wide as possible, it would have been hard pressed to find a more efficient way than to have listeners memorize it. By the time Protestants reversed this by having the Bible read in the native tongue, it was too late – people had long been removed from a sense that oral tradition was important and did not derive as much benefit from it as the early converts would have.

When studying texts that captured something originally transmitted orally – like the epics or the Vedas – it is important to remember the way it was meant to be experienced. Texts cannot reproduce the intonations, emotions, or even the feeling of the sounds as it was recited. Reading a translation produces even more problems, depending on the mood, biases, and vocabulary of the translator. The difference between reading a text of orally transmitted material and hearing it being passed down is equivalent to that between the singing of a song and reading a lyric sheet – the two experiences cannot be equated. The importance and beauty of the Vedas may not be clear to people who read them today – and too often people consider such works important simply because of their age. The same is true of the bulk of the Iliad and all those passages people tend to skip over – the lists of names and minor fights that were stirringly recited from the mouth of the storyteller. This is the most basic issue in understanding teachings passed down through the centuries. College lectures are somewhat similar, maintaining a minimal connection between people and old traditions. Unfortunately, the goal for students in such lectures is to take as complete a set of notes as possible, and students often skip lectures regularly as textbooks replace professors. The goal of oral tradition is to remember the teachings, so that they are fresh in the mind and can be readily applied to daily life.

The state of modern memory and the way it hinders people cannot be overstated. Consider how writing is relied on to preserve knowledge, and how people are actually encouraged by this not to memorize what they are supposed to learn. Even worse is the archiving that people do through diaries and all the other substitutes for memories. Failing to remember ideas presented by others is one thing, needing devices to record one's own life is quite another. People are encouraged not to remember. The prevalent image in the culture of education is the student cramming the night before a test. There is no expectation that a person can remember the main points of straightforward course material for the few months that make up a semester. What, then, is the point of trying to teach people in such a culture? Needless to say, this cultural attitude leads to a diminishment in the importance of teachers, and people have a distorted view that a good teacher is one that entertains.

How can the modern era's catchword – progress – be propelled in this situation? Inevitably, this will lead to stagnation, since the system cannot be sustained if its rudiments are forgotten. There may always be geniuses, but to sustain a system, especially in a democracy where decisions are made by the majority, the greatest number of people as possible must have the mental tools to understand a complex situation. Perspective requires memory. What good are brilliant minds if no one understands what they are saying, or what the implications of their words are? For that matter, what about spiritual masters – can they successfully communicate higher ideals to people, or will they always become forms of entertainment? In this world of mass media in which any person with sufficient charisma can get his name known, it is increasingly difficult to tell who truly believes, understands, and has experience in what they are teaching, and if some are merely selling a product. It is easier to take advantage of a person without memory or perspective, or a lack of even high school knowledge of math, science, and history. If knowledge is power, it makes sense that those with power would seek to limit the education of others.

Perspective requires the ability to contain a wide range of ideas in the mind and understand how those ideas interact with each other, and the everyday world. A lack of this created a skewed view of history, with a bias towards just a few days ago. This is very convenient for politicians, who only need to address those issue that they remind people of. It also creates a bias against spirituality, at least those forms of spirituality that were not formed in the last few years, or refreshed in the minds of people every Sunday. The irony is that we, today, need sharp memories even more than those living two thousand years ago did, partly because writing has allowed for the widespread sharing of information. There is more knowledge to sort out and process. The problem is that there is too much information for anyone to digest in one lifetime. Most people give up on their curiosity and take too much for granted, including their dissatisfaction.

The goal of those who are aware of this dynamic, then, should not be to stop writing. Rather, people should cultivate their memory to compliment reading or writing. Avoiding the laziness that comes with externalizing memory will be rewarded later in life, since the more often knowledge is recalled and connected to other information, the better it will be retained. The greater the information a person had at his or her disposal at any given moment, the more informed a decision that person can make to deal with a situation or a spiritual crisis. Some might argue otherwise, but I cannot help but feel that they are simply overwhelmed by the useless information. It is necessary to make a conscious decision about what to remember, and those things should all be valuable tools, not the television guide. Practical knowledge can give a person confidence in the face of adversity and stress. There is perhaps nothing so stressful as moving very fast and getting nowhere, which is the basic condition of most of the population in the modern world, as long as we can dismiss the notion that collecting material wealth qualifies as getting somewhere.

It is incorrect to say that short memories and lack of perspective in the modern era are only caused by our use of written tradition instead of oral tradition, but the fact that we have mostly abandoned the latter has definitely played a significant part. And if some steps are taken to reverse the current trends – for instance, if the culture encourages students to believe that they actually have to listen to teachers and remember what is said instead of cramming the night before – then I believe you will see those students become, on average, more patient and less stressed. If an individual in regular life learns to listen and process information, a similar effect should be expected.

However, the actual trend is in the opposite direction. In the past forty years, the world has become increasingly visual, and read less. Visual culture is useful for advertisers but little else, since the sources of visual tradition – television in particular – rarely convey deep understanding. It is suited to the impatient, hectic, and stressful modern age, but not appropriate for instilling patience or relieving stress. Compared to the way people today learn, and have tradition passed down to them, reading and writing would be a great improvement. Writing is actually fading away steadily, and reading has declined to the point children have to be coaxed to pick up a book. So, the criticism of written tradition's domination has to be taken in context – and the current context is that we are in the midst of another shift in the way tradition is passed down, making an examination of the last shift even more important.

Whatever the modern day issues, the gap in the two traditions will unfailingly affect the way people understand ancient belief systems. It is a cultural element that is rarely considered, especially in relationship to spirituality and the type of spiritual practices that develop. To our benefit, we have the opportunity to use a mixed system, putting the best of both systems to work. It would be a shame to ignore this opportunity, and even worse to loose touch with both traditions in the face of visual communication.

Perspective

The Attraction of the New and Polarization of the Old

"Science fiction yesterday, fact today, obsolete tomorrow."
Otto O. Binder

Some might ask, after reading the discussion of oral and written tradition, why did people make the switch? Why, for that matter, did ancient peoples convert to Christianity? There is an odd idea called progress that is attached to the modern era, but is also fundamental to one interpretation of history. Progress, in this context, means the acceptance of the new as necessarily better than the old. Needless to say, it is a problematic notion at best, and at worst wrong. This way of understanding history, commonly called the Whig interpretation, named after the party in England that emphasized progress in its debates, frames the stretch of human development from the agricultural revolution twelve thousand years ago onward in terms of continual progress. This view is inviting mainly because it is a satisfying illusion of recent history – since in the past century the forces supporting progress have overwhelmed those that emphasized and defended tradition.

Needless to say, this is a massive distortion in the understanding of the past, and of time. Thankfully, it is no longer believed without qualification, but there will always be a Whig undercurrent in the study of history. The new has always fascinated people. It draws some people towards it, while inspiring both rational and irrational fear in others. If there seems to be some sort of progress to history, it is because the proponents of progress emphasize the former and dismiss the rational element in the latter. There has consistently been some pressure towards the novelty, putting strain on those who, in opposition to this, are attempting to learn or preserve either the spirituality or ideas of older times. Sometimes, the defense of the old is successful, or even too successful. Note that this is not a battle between the past and the future, which would be nonsense. This all occurs within reality – in the now. It is actually the struggle between two interpretations of the past, each attempting to mold the future.

We see this everywhere, and in both organized religion and alternative spirituality, with the struggle causing no end of trouble. The way to avoid getting caught by this dynamic is to reject being polarized into one side or the other of the duality. It is too easy to make older ideas absurd by reinventing them as the complete opposite of anything new. In recent times, the new has not had to defend itself, but people can take to absurd extremes simply by trusting every new idea – or product – that comes along wholeheartedly. Each side attacks the other, and tries to restrict the freedom of choice. This ends up being destructive on both sides, because the traditional is not allowed to absorb the best of the new ideas, making it unsuited to the changing cultural context, and the new ways are not tempered by the wisdom of the old.

To show that this dynamic is nothing new, I will begin by making observations about the conversion of the classical world to Christianity. By the time of Christ, Rome had in its possession all of the land surrounding the Mediterranean. The Empire was notoriously tolerant of different religions, but Christianity posed a special problem. Christians actively sought to convert others, and they defied Caesar by refusing to pledge allegiance to him. The Jews also did not swear allegiance to

Perspective

Caesar, and for the same reason – the Bible's teachings dictate that humans should swear allegiance only to God, but they kept to themselves and certainly did not attempt to convert. To the Roman leadership, which after the fall of the Republic was rarely stable, Christianity was a new phenomenon deliberately designed to undermine the authority of the emperor.

The response to Christianity included sporadic persecution and occasional acceptance, a complicated response due to the fact that some senators, and more aristocratic wives, had converted to the new religion. Their interest in it mostly rested in its novelty, and the secrecy with which its most important tenets were kept. If there is anything more compelling than something fresh and new, it is a mystery. Ultimately, of course, the emperor Constantine himself converted – albeit on his deathbed – signaling the end of the old Roman religion.

This may seem a coarse and simplistic way to discuss the initial triumph of the world's largest religion, but it is precisely what occurred, with no more complex motive necessary. There were no underlying struggles that led people to flock to Christianity, except perhaps for individual dissatisfaction. Roman religious beliefs had Greek backing – the highest authority available – and faced only the normal philosophical issues theist systems face. Besides, the many festivals and benefits coming out of the Roman pantheon regularly reminded people of the state belief system, probably even more frequently than every seven days. It is safe to say that, until the individual reaches the ultimate in self-development, he will always be dissatisfied. So, it should come as no surprise that, if old ways have not produced satisfaction, or if new ways claim to do so more quickly and efficiently, people move on to the new. This is not the only reason the new tends to be attractive, but it certainly applies to the Romans.

Time and the Human Condition

When Christians sought to proselytize outside the core of the Roman Empire, though, they faced unique problems in each area. In general, the early Christians adapted their message to each new culture. Open-mindedness was necessary, because outside of Rome, cultures had much more rigid systems of belief and took a great deal of convincing. For instance, to those tribes who still employed sacrifices to appease the gods, the Christians explained that Christ was a great and honorable man who made the ultimate self-sacrifice so that no more sacrifices would be required. This explanation, then, made sense to the tribes. All their attempts had not helped them against the Romans, so they had an interest in new ways. And frankly speaking, though they might not have thought this way, sacrifices were a ghastly business, while the idea of Christ's self-sacrifice had a unique beauty to it.

The conversions did not happen overnight, but considering the bloodless way it was managed in the early years, the spread of Christianity may appear striking, but not after considering the way society is managed today. Consumer culture itself depends on novelty to sell. Fashions might be the most obvious example of this, but every new subculture that has developed since the late Sixties has been absorbed into the mainstream because it is something new that can be sold. Aside from fashions and subcultures, computer technology shows the same trend. There is a push to upgrade to new versions even when the older technology is actually more stable. And since the attraction of the new is required for the creation of wealth, there is an active attempt to promote the idea that newer is better. It can be seen in advertisements all the time, while there are very few ads that use the test of time as a selling point. We have been through over a century of 'newer is better' in America and, though recently the defense of tradition has grown much fiercer, there is no sign that the business tactic is any less successful.

Perspective

The prevalence of this message – conveyed by all the new forms of visual media – has generated an irrational disregard for old ideas in industrial nations and within all cities. The trend within cities dates back all the way to Rome. Port cities are notorious for their ability to pick up any and every idea that comes along, as was true of the port town which fed Rome, which was actually more receptive to odd ideas than the great city itself. The sheer mass of people living in close quarters demands that each person distinguish him or herself, to outline individuality. There is an old German saying to the effect that city air makes men free. In a way, the propensity for every new idea to be picked up ensures nonconformity and a sense of freedom.

The typical contrast is the small town or village, in which everyone knows each other and there is only the countryside around. In the small rural town, peer pressure stifles attempts at novelty and people are expected to obey the dominant norms. There is nothing so impossible as pursuing alternative spirituality in a small town that is adamantly obeying a major religion. On the other hand, a small town with similar spiritual interests to a person can be a boon, providing a helpful, supportive environment completely unlike the alien and aloof atmosphere of the city and suburbs. It should be noted that American schools, especially high school, can behave somewhat like small towns, so that many people living in the cities have some idea of what rural towns are like. Each environment has its benefits and weaknesses.

The increasing emphasis on progress is very much related to the city's need for novelty and increasing city population. Urban population surpassed rural in the United Stated in 1920. Not surprisingly, what we now call consumer culture – characterized by massive advertising and use of credit – began in the twenties. It took some time before a reaction to this developed – mainly thanks to the Great Depression and the Second World War. This allowed the idea of progress to gain significant ground among the middle class, which had recovered by 1950. In that time, scientists became authorities for everything, science could solve all problems, and every technological advance was a triumph against communism. The fight against communism provided the vehicle for traditionalist reactions – everything against the norm was dubbed "communist" and the nation dipped into an uncharacteristic conformity. The two polarized sides battled in the Sixties, and it seemed like new cultural values, like racial equality and gender equality, won out. Under the aegis of Ronald Reagan, though, the eighties allowed traditionalists to gain some voice. By the turn of the century the two sides have become polarized beyond anything the nation has ever seen, and the dialogue is explicitly about traditional religious values and the need to defend them.

    This polarization is destructive because it prevents people from seeing the gray areas, where compromises can be made. The population is actually encouraged not to be reasonable. In any given situation, there are more than two points of view, more than two options, and the best course lies somewhere between the extremes. An 'either you're with us or against us' attitude is certainly not one that is compatible with enlightened spiritual values, and has caused nations and organized religions no end of trouble.

    The key, then, is to try to avoid the mistake on an individual level. This is easier said than done, but it is not necessary to keep a perfect balance. The most simple step an individual can take is to avoid being afraid. Fear is, after all, the initial impulse of most people when dealing with the past, and interpretations of it. Don't shy away from analyzing ancient texts, and don't miss the chance to put useful tools like

Perspective

computers to work. In the hands of people with a constructive purpose, ancient wisdom and modern technology can come together magnificently, and that constructive purpose can be more efficiently applied to molding the future. How this is managed, and to what extent, is purely a matter of individual preference. The key is making sure that everything contributes to personal development rather than detracting from it.

Time and the Human Condition

Why have the illusion of money, but not one of world peace?

I posed this as a rhetorical question in the introduction, but will here answer it because there is an instructive answer. The discussion of oral and written tradition concluded that our perspective is growing narrower. This truncated perspective subsequently inflates the importance of recent events and experience, while significantly deflating our interest in lessons from times long past. If we understate this a bit, it means that we place more emphasis on what we learn in our lives and experience, while dismissing the knowledge gained by our predecessors.

When discussing world peace, it is first of all obvious that there are no precedents – no models to follow. Of course, the search for models is hampered by the fact that the people of the world have only been mutually aware of each other for a little over a hundred years, if that. But as examined before, lack of precedent would not be a hindrance if everyone, or perhaps even just an influential minority, believed world peace was possible. The most significant bar to the idea, though certainly not the only one, is the simple fact that the generation that has been in power until recently has been the generation that fought the Second World War. Or as they not-so-humbly dub themselves, the Greatest Generation.

This would not be a problem if perspectives were broader, and the lessons of antiquity were respected. Here is the old lesson, put simply: violence cannot solve problems. Here is

Perspective

the lesson we took out of World War Two: violence can solve problems. Let us examine the logic step-by-step.

The First World War confirmed the old lesson, and horrified Europe into a resolve that it should never happen again – leading to structures like the League of Nations, which ended up ineffective because the United States failed to ratify it. There were a few in power, though, who had been desensitized of the horror through the four years, and in the aftermath of the war were merely angry. That is one reason why violence cannot solve problems – there is too much residual resentment on all sides, and this will lead to further conflict. It is a lesson that was long understood, and has for some reason been recently forgotten – no nation will truly welcome an invading foreign army, the people only cheer for fear of getting shot otherwise. At the end of World War I, the underlying anger blinded the leaders of England and France. They knew that the Germans would be resentful, but did not care about the resentment that their punitive measures would breed, and did not think that the resentment might lead to a new war. When more level-headed observers saw the Treaty of Versailles, many immediately concluded that there another war would be the natural result. One such observer actually concluded that there would be another war in twenty years – the exact amount of time between the two world wars.

But people still came out of the First World War with a clear sense that war was futile, and with the intent to avoid it at all costs. Then, as if some "loki-esque" trickster deity saw the opportunity, the world spawned two dictators who believed that it was the place of great peoples to conquer as much of the world as they could. Hitler and Mussolini took advantage of the pacifistic environment in the twenties and thirties, and the rest of Europe held true to the old lesson, culminating in the Munich Agreement – which basically handed over much of Czechoslovakia over to Hitler, so long as peace would be maintain. We have all learned, and some of us have perhaps heard, Neville Chamberlain's "Peace in Our Time" speech, so there is no need to go into it further. We also need not delve too far into the consequences of this resolute devotion to peace – the Second World War.

The point is that the Second World War taught people that trying to keep peace through negotiations was pointless – it only gave time for the enemy to get stronger. There is a collective amnesia concerning the lessons of the First World War, and today war is considered to be both the easiest and the best solution. Leaders need only to do one thing to gain support for a war – compare the enemy leader to Hitler. And no matter how ludicrous the comparison may be, people believe it. Part of this may be the failure of education, but it is, in fact, because they want to believe it. The generation that lived through the Second World War learned early on to think of diplomacy in a "good versus evil" way. Thus, after Hitler was destroyed, the Communists were quickly labeled "evil." And the trend has continued. It is comfortable to have such a view of international relations, because it gives confidence to any choice. After all, if we are the good guys, we can do no wrong.

In short, the experiences of the World War Two generation have ensured that world peace has never even been seriously considered. There are no efforts to that end, and it remains an idea fit for comedy – the first thing you ask the genie for when you rub the lamp. This is not to say that if the Second World War had not occurred as it did, we would have world peace, but take a look at the real results. The twentieth century was bloodier than the rest of human history combined, and the twenty-first century is not shaping up much different. Clearly, the hope for peace is an important idea, and needs to be fostered. Instead, it seems like the people have required a constant enemy to call evil. This has not been true only of Americans, but is present around the world, and generates a great deal of mutual resentment. The good versus evil view of politics, Hitler's destructive legacy, has made peaceful negotiation an obsolete option.

But how does this connect to the illusion of money? First, it should be understood that money is not the only medium of exchange. In many pre-industrial societies, in fact, it was acceptable to pay even taxes in kind – with livestock or other goods – and most farmers required the ability to pay for things with their products in order to survive. That is normally called the barter system, and reflects the individual values people might place on items. The use of money, or specie (gold or silver), benefits the merchant class, since it facilitates the exchange of goods, and merchants can assign higher prices than would be possible under the barter system. There are many customers in the marketplace, and the abstract nature of money allows a merchant to coax people to pay more for a good than they would have when paying in kind. The divide in the perception of money, from the old distrust of it as a merchant manipulation to our current dependence on the monetary system, solidified in the twenties with the start of consumer culture and the rise of the merchant class as the majority. But even with that early materialistic revolution, there was inadequate trust in the value of money, and this shaky trust, and distrust in the banks and their speculations, developed into the Great Depression of the thirties.

Money still had to be backed by gold – though, of course, gold also only has value because of a collective illusion. At least gold looks impressive. The final change came when money was no longer backed by anything except the currency exchange. After the Second World War, money quickly gained the support it needed to stand on its own, up to the seventies, when other nations started backing their currencies with the U.S. dollar. The key to the difference between the thirties and the sixties can be found in the fifties. In the 1950s, communism was the new enemy – the great evil against which the United States had to stand as the bastion of the good. As a result, any questioning of capitalistic or materialistic goals was considered not only wrong or distasteful, but evil and criminal. That the dollar could suddenly stand on its own should come as no surprise in such a climate, and thanks to both the temperament and other factors. One of these other factors was what President Eisenhower called the military-industrial complex – the United States government had learned in the Second World War that warfare, when conducted outside of the country, has economic benefits – and Eisenhower hoped the government could exercise proper restraint, but his warnings went mostly unheeded. America experienced an unparalleled economic boom through the fifties and sixties that has not been matched by anything before or since, which was followed by the recovery of Europe in the sixties and seventies, and this capped confidence in the economic system.

People had faith in money, and none in peace. The story is not quite so simple, but at its core, this simple sentence encompasses the reasons behind the mindset of the world today. And the reason behind that sense of confidence can be found in what the generation involved itself consider its defining event – the Second World War. Now, given that, I know what people in the United States might think: the Vietnam War generation is starting to take power, certainly it has a different, though admittedly similarly narrow, perspective? That is the trouble with narrow perspectives – there is no benefit to them. In fact, the Vietnam generation has developed some very interesting ideas after having the Greatest Generation's version of history hammered into it.

The Vietnam generation, on average, lacks any knowledge of the Second World War – again, short memories, written and visual tradition – except for the vital fact that it was a war or good against evil, and that the evil was Hitler. So comparing enemies to Hitler will still have the desired effect. And, while there were certainly massive protests during the Vietnam War, almost all members of the generation either did not participate, or have disavowed the ideas of the time, dismissing it all as generational rebellion. Now that the generation is in power, the overwhelming attitude is in favor of suppressing all those things that the generation enjoyed in its youth – drugs, free speech, and protest. The first of these might be justified, but to have the government enforcing the idea instead of leaving it up to the individual, is against the principles of both democracy and republicanism. If we accept that the government can ban the use of drugs because of its indirect impact on society, we would have to accept any argument made where the government presumes to know more than the sovereign people about what is best, and ultimately those interests will serve more what is best for the class that controls the government than the people as a whole. The government was limited to the powers listed in the Constitution for a reason. As far as free speech and protest go, the Vietnam generation learned early that these two really can cause trouble for those in power, and now that they are in power, the tolerance for such disruptions guaranteed by the First Amendment has diminished.

This primarily rises out of a lack of perspective. With more perspective, the government and people of the country would be more concerned with the loss of their rights, which were so ardently fought for by their ancestors. Fear, whether rational or irrational, leads to a demand for safety, and a limitation of freedom. It also encourages people to react rashly instead of in a well-considered manner, and rash decisions are more likely to be violent, while peaceful negotiations always require careful thought.

Naturally, war is not always avoidable. Because these dynamics, and limitations on perspective, affect everyone, it

Time and the Human Condition

is difficult for any one nation to take a peaceful stance and still feel completely secure. Today, we simply do not have the patience, necessary understanding, and depth of memory to conceive of all options before resorting to war. The aftermath and consequences of war are left unexamined until after the war has ended, since foresight is also undermined by lack of perspective.

The direction of this discussion should be fairly clear, but I can state the ultimate conclusion to be drawn from all of this: there cannot be world peace until people in general have a level of perspective unmatched in human history – because no time in history so far has been completely peaceful. In fact, it might be the case that a sense of time as close to universal consciousness as possible in this world might be necessary for the ideal to be realized. Consider some of the more recent enlightened figures – Gandhi and Martin Luther King, for instance – and you will see that they are unfailingly more resistant to fear, adamant about not using force to solve problem, always speak with the weight of centuries, and have the kind of broad perspective that is essential in negotiation. In all cases, those figures should be the model for the ideal, and all of their key characteristics should be considered hand-in-hand, such that seeking one of them will also bring a person further on the road to the others.

Unfortunately, the models people are exposed to in modern society – those they find in movies and other media – all reflect the kind of mindset that sees war as a viable and simple solution to most political problems, and sees diplomacy as a sign of weakness. An entire genre of movies is dedicated to glorifying war and warriors, while the only a handful of movies glorify peacemakers. Dreams of world peace have no impact because the culture, educated by recent history, rejects it not only as impossible but also an invitation to dictators. Culture creates a feedback loop ensuring that without a major shift in thinking, the existing attitudes will only increase in potency.

Part 4
Applying Perspective

Time and the Human Condition

Key Aspects In Applying Perspective

The current state of the world, with its constant interactions and dynamic influences, has affectively made perspectives gained by individual experience and culture less encompassing and more diffuse. There is so much to deal with, it is difficult for cultures, much less individuals, to adapt to or understand anything at adequate depth. Just as groups of people living in close proximity to each other necessitated some level of cultural perspective to facilitate mutual understanding, swift communication has brought cultures into close proximity to each other. Without recourse to broader perspective, these cultures will come into conflict. The bombardment of new ideas brought by the modern age of communication simply does not allow calm interaction unless cultures can somehow rise above their own ideas and actively try to avoid confrontation or the use of coercive manipulation.

In nations like the United States, in which cultures are brought together in a single political unit, the idea of culture wars has already been coined and the more vicious battles have been fought since 1980. The issue of immigration is always a flashpoint in such culture wars, because it threatens to bring people in who will tip opinions in one direction or another. The issues being contested change over time, and in the recent times of intense strife revolved around abortion, evolution versus creationism, the drug war, welfare, homosexuality, gun control, and a slew of other points of contention. Each of these issues have far greater implications than are normally discussed when people fight over them. For instance, the actual logic behind the abortion issue is a struggle concerning the place of women in society, which is one of the major focuses of the modern culture wars. The fight is framed in terms of abortion, but looking deeply into the logic of both polarized sides, and the history of organizations on the two sides, reveals why this issue has grown so intense. As another example, the fight over the teaching of evolution has nothing to do with how the human race really developed, and everything to do with establishing which has preeminence – scientific conclusions or religious faith. This particular cultural issue has a long history, dating at least to the 1920s. At that time, the temperance movement had just won the major cultural struggle –the prohibition of alcohol – and that movement was in large part a proxy for the struggle between Protestants and immigrants who were mostly Catholic. Without the widespread use of at least the historical level of perspective, there will be increasingly frequent conflict at the cultural level, both within and across national boundaries. People will choose sides without even fully realizing why the conflict exists.

As previously noted, the broader levels of perception tend to be inaccessible to the bulk of the population. However, this is not due to the inability of people to understand or synthesize, but rather due to a lack of focus on more complex levels of thought in education and limits on the free time needed to think things through. In its best aspect, the modern world is defined by expanding education, expanding participation in politics, and equality before the law. These developments, which defined modernity, were the product of a few brilliant minds during the seventeenth and eighteenth centuries, and have merely been put into practice and expanded upon since. Further developments along the same lines have been slow in coming, but that is only the natural complacency that comes with a system functioning tolerably and without detrimental disruptions.

Time and the Human Condition

All of these modern innovation, though the product of a few minds, must be defended and maintained by all those who benefit from them. However, while education, politics, and law have been refined to encompass more people with greater equality than every before, their quality has been diminished. This is particularly clear in education, and despite the greater extent of knowledge, less and less of it is being taught to students early – at least in the Western schools out of which the innovators came. The fact that the dissemination of abstract knowledge is currently reserved for the universities has fed into the trend toward specialization, since only English and Mathematics are emphasized in grade school, and there is inadequate time and too much pressure in college for people to study a true breadth of subjects there. The problem with specialization is that it limits the perspective that can be gained through the synthesis of knowledge. While eventually, there will have to be specialization for the individual to be productive in society, the earlier it occurs, the more limitations are placed on the individual. In addition, to avoid limitations there should always be an attitude favoring curiosity and the synthesis of knowledge gained from that curiosity.

The section that follows will examine education in some more detail, further emphasizing the need for a style of education which encourages the development of perspective, perhaps by encouraging student interpretations rather than the simple regurgitation currently required of students. After that, government will be in the spotlight, as the way party politics tends to oversimplify issues into two positions, and therefore disenfranchise those who have a third view of things, is taken to task. It is one thing for a person to have a limited scope of the issues because of a lack of knowledge or time to consider things properly; it is far less acceptable for a person to have a limited scope of the issues because those limited views are all he or she is given to choose from.

Applying Perspective

The final section on applying perspective deals with law and the difference between justice and order, with justice requiring broad understanding of the law and flexible interpretation depending on the dilemmas a case might pose, and order requiring strict enforcement with no consideration for the particulars of a case. Order is emphasized when there is simply no time to get a full picture of the case, and examine it from every possible viewpoint, while justice should be the goal of every society that is not in the midst of bombardment or other disruption that would make the normal processes of law impossible.

Time and the Human Condition

On Education

> *"Men are born ignorant, not stupid. They are made stupid by Education."*
> Bertrand Russell

There has to be a way for the individual to expand his or her own perspective, and sense of the universe. To some extent, criticisms are cast in the hope that the collective intelligence will look into matters and come up with solutions. A few areas in particular, however, should be particular targets for change. One of those areas, education, has to change before all others, because it has so much influence on the way we think – and rarely in the ways educators intend it to. In some regions of the world, education is tightly controlled and is used specifically for indoctrination. The democratic world can correctly use these as an example of how much more open to discussion our own schools are, but should also see what to avoid, and head in the opposite direction in search of better education. If indoctrination is the example to avoid, then ever-broader understanding and introductions to a variety of ideas is what should be sought.

Education was originally meant to inculcate children with the values of the established society at an early, impressionable age. While we have moved on to a more enlightened understanding of education, some sense of the early system still remains. They were, and still often are, made to know one interpretation of history – focusing on the history of their nation, one language, and one understanding of ethics and morality, despite the diversity of their origins. None of this is necessarily a problem. Language is a tool for communication, and it is therefore best that there should be some common ground within the society. To what extent children actually learn history, they might as well learn the history of the land around them to start with. The real problem is two-fold: the way the initial motives of mandatory education limit interpretations of what is taught, and the fact that those initial motives still determine what children are not taught.

Let us look back through time to examine the initial motives and why they might cause problems. In the United States, mandatory education became popular when, at the end of the nineteenth and start of the twentieth century, immigrants started arriving from Eastern Europe with ideas that were considered foreign and dangerous. Until that group of immigrants started arriving, the nation was dominantly Protestant with only a very small Catholic population. The Eastern Europeans were overwhelmingly Catholic or Jewish. But the religious issue was only part of the concern. All new immigrants were automatically thought of as anarchists and labor agitators, because at the time, the labor question was the single most significant issue in domestic affairs. It was easy for management to blame all labor agitation on immigrants, and to exploit the racism of the time. The single most commonly cited reason for the lack of a strong socialist or labor party in America is the success business leaders had in dividing workers along ethnic lines, fostering hostility between them. Immigrants fueled criticism and animosity by adamantly maintaining their own language within isolated communities, carving out little versions of their own lands instead of becoming integrated into America, supporting the illusion that they were trying to undermine the American Way.

So, education became mandatory for everyone under a certain age to convert these people to the American system. The rhetoric was more vicious than this logical explanation might make it out to be – the education reforms occurred at a time when Social Darwinism (the idea that evolution operates on both social classes and races, with lower classes and other races actually lesser human beings) was considered fact, and eugenics (dealing with social problems by preventing potentially problematic people – and many included the poor and immigrants in this group – from procreating) a good idea. Tight immigration laws were thought necessary to limit the pollution of the gene pool. This was the age of progressivism, and America could not risk all the backward ideas immigrants were bound to bring, so they had to be converted or prevented from entering the country.

Ultimately the decision had its benefits, but the original motives were not to inform or to broaden the perspectives of youth, and rather to put children on a single established path, and to limit their perspective to what is deemed acceptable to the most powerful people in the country. That is, the people in the country that would most benefit from teaching children to follow the status quo, and have the most to lose from deviant ideas. Since that time, the state of education has grown steadily broader, but the foundations of the system remain evident in the way students are taught today, especially with the interpretation of history and literature throughout the lower grades, and sometimes on into high school. Though there are some outgoing schools and teachers attempt to push the limits, and to give students a more varied and intellectually stimulating education, this is not the dominant trend.

In America, the current push to improve the state of education revolves around accountability – an abstract concept that seems to demand that students do well on standardized tests. These tests focus solely on English and Mathematics, and while the latter subject is certainly a necessity and easily testable, the former can often be subjective. Also, there is a range of skills beyond these base-level subjects that are the real measure of learning. English and Mathematics are two languages in which to communicate information, while there is also Art, Music, and other languages which are simply too subjective to test, or are considered not worth testing. These languages should also be mastered at an early age. By high school, the education system should be interested only in how the languages are put to use, and it should be assumed that all students who have reached high school have already developed a grasp on at least one language, and will specialize in the subjects where that language is most used. If this assumption cannot be made, then students are being forced through the system without being ready to move on.

Part of the problem might be the expectation that education can be matched directly to age, and that a certain level of thought can be expected from everyone of the same age. Clearly this is not valid, so at the risk of demoralizing them, students should only be moved on to the next grade if they are ready for far greater tasks than was expected of them in the grade that they are in. Frankly, a student's lack of readiness for the course material in the higher grade is usually more demoralizing than being held back would be. Grade levels should be completely independent from age, and there should be no assumption in the society that a certain grade naturally corresponds to a certain age. Eliminating such assumptions should reduce the demoralization that might occur, though it might not suit neat bureaucracies. In fact, if the system works as intended, close to half of all students should be refused advancement at least once in their schooling, and the sense that this is something many students have to overcome will also reduce the stigma of being held back. Needless to say, exceptional students should be moved on faster, if it is deemed that they are prepared for it. Under no circumstances should either exceptional students or problematic students be removed to special classes, like honors classes. Any isolation limits the perspectives of students.

Another part of the problem is that students are not made aware of the practical application of what they are learning, despite the fact that they often ask. If a teacher cannot explain why it is important to learn a topic, then the topic should not be taught. Otherwise, students should always be taught to readily apply their learning, even at the primary levels of education. With mathematics, this is easy to accomplish with real world examples, but even in an abstract subject like history it is readily possible. In history classes, students should, by high school, be experienced in applying what lessons they themselves have concluded from the facts of history onto contemporary events. Also, they should be experienced in looking at documents and art from different periods in history, and using the facts of history to draw conclusions about the document. Clearly, there are ways to show the practical application of any subject, otherwise the subjects would not be taught in the first place.

The discussion above centers on combating the continuing attempts to normalize education, which is a remnant of the initial motive of mandatory education – to normalize the society and facilitate the absorption of immigrants into the dominant culture. If the tendency moves away from the normalization that standardized testing brings and towards emphasizing the application of learning, a diversification of interpretation of the subject matter will likely result. There are only a few languages that can be tested by standardized means, but many applications, and it is in those applications that diversity of knowledge can be found. But there are also subjects that the current American education system simply fails to cover, and some of these subjects might enrich the perspectives of the students.

If we want to add subjects that will enrich the perspectives of students, then dealing with perspectives in space would be good place to start, and geography would fill the role admirably.

Applying Perspective

Why is geography no longer considered an essential part of education, as a separate course? Certainly it should be, since it is impossible to begin to understand world events without it. Geography is not solely map work, but can also include studies in climate, cultures, details about vegetation, and basic facts about different areas of the world. There is nothing more absurd than making claims about people in a country, or about a country's politics, without being able to find the country on a map. It would be best if people learned something about cultures around the world before hearing news stories, which will often involve the worst elements of those cultures and therefore unintentionally inspire a skewed view. For even greater perspective in space, astronomy could use greater emphasis in the basic science courses required of students when they enter high school. In the discussion of astronomy, the vast distances involved and the current attempts to explore the expanse of space should be made clear – simply having students learn the names of planets will not convey the importance of the universe beyond Earth's atmosphere.

But the idea of perspective that we have been tangling with in previous sections is in relation to time. For the broadest sense of time, physics can be further emphasized. It would be an immense improvement if the principles of classical physics discussed in this book, and the theories of relativity in particular, were required knowledge for students graduating from high school. Perspectives of time narrowed down from the theoretical to the practical, however, suggests the need for attention to how history is taught.

If a country insists on teaching its own history while minimizing discussion of others, it would be best if that history stretches thousands of years, if only to give a sense of the vast expanse of people and ideas that have come before. If this is impossible, then there are a number of ways to solve the problem. All Western nations, or nations coming out of

Time and the Human Condition

Western colonialism, can easily include study of the Greeks and Romans, and perhaps the key theories of the era between 1500 and 1800 A.D., all of which would be critical to understanding the modern histories of those countries. The study of the classics was standard in both Britain and the United States until the 1920s, when the democratization of the schools meant that standards were deliberately lowered, in theory to accommodate the diversity of the massive influx. Also, mathematics and sciences became popular, and they displaced the old focus of higher learning, which had been on history and ancient philosophy. China, India, and most of the Pacific Rim can boast a deep enough history to satisfy the necessities of perspective. In the Middle East, there should be, and often is, an awareness of the full history of the land stretching from Egypt to Iran, which in 3000 B.C. served as the cradle of civilization and has had a continuous history since then. The greatest problem will be in North and South America, as the modern cultures clearly lack a connection to the Native American past and, with the exception of the United States and Canada, have been alienated from European history thanks to the legacy of colonialism.

The problem is teaching history at an intelligent enough level that students can benefit from it. In many areas, there is a growing disrespect for education for two reasons – it is perceived as having no connection with material success, and it is perceived as hypocritical. The hypocrisy stems mainly from deliberate misinformation – in America this can be seen in the rosy picture painted of the interaction between settlers and Native Americans during elementary school, in middle school the biased way world cultures are painted in the history textbooks, and in high school the explanation of the Constitution and the powers allowed to the government, which stands in contrast to the actual functioning of the government. The whole problem has become a feedback loop – education has become irrelevant, and students come in with a lack of respect for the system, making it even more irrelevant. Even worse, society itself does not value anything that schools can teach, so that even if schools started providing a broad range of perspectives, the damage has already been done and students will continue to aim for mediocrity. After all, the smartest people in the world are far from being the richest, many of the wealthiest did not even complete their education, and wealth is what society values.

If there is any facet of society in which it would make sense to start a broadening of perspectives, it should be in education. Granted, altering education to provide the potential for understanding will not make students more prepared for life in society as it is right now, but it might give them ideas for how to change society for the better in the future. Any process of this sort will take a long time, but we have not really considered how best to improve our system – no such discussion is in the public discourse. The ultimate solution need not resemble the suggestions made above, but there should at least be opinions and debates on such an important issue. Education is an important place to improve because it is often where bad habits first develop. For instance, the habit of regurgitating the teacher's opinion to get a good grade is a classic bad habit, but perhaps the ideal way to graduate with minimal trouble. It is not only lamentable for the suppression of original thought, but it also fosters mindless obedience to authority, which is precisely what the Enlightenment in the seventeenth and eighteenth century struggled to rescue us from. In addition, it makes sense that, if we are going to demand that all children under sixteen attend school, it should be worth their while. They can be provided with tools that, without education, would be unavailable to them.

Time and the Human Condition

On Government and Party Politics

"Government, even in its best state, is but a necessary evil; in its worst state, an intolerable one."
Thomas Paine

As they do in all the other areas of human life, time and perspective have a major impact on the way we govern ourselves. In medieval times, the most important link to the past for politics was the family tree of the king. Most political conflicts began with one king, with a superior fighting force waiting to be deployed, trying to find some way, however distant in time or relationship, that he could legitimately lay hereditary claim to the lands of a weaker king. When history was rewritten in medieval times, the king's family tree was being redrawn. A succession claim was all the reason that was required for war. Survival was still tied to the land, and most landowners were subsistence farmers, so a king had a duty to increase the size of his lands to better provide for his people. But Europeans consider those times the Dark Ages, a void between the light of the Greco-Romans and the Enlightenment, so let us see what we have today that makes us think we have progressed.

There is no question that, on average, more people are involved in the political process than ever before. That is the most common change that will be noted, and it is definitely a fortunate one. However, whether involvement leads to impact is another matter. The real impact is still in the hands of the wealthy – the modern equivalent of the nobility – in most nations. There are a number of key signs of this, and they all involve catering to the varied perspectives of the population. After all, if millions of people vote, each should have a different shade of understanding, and unique experiences that inform his or her decisions. So, any country that asks its voters to decide between one, two, or three parties is really not giving its population any choice at all. How can the ideas of millions of people be distilled into one, two, or three collected points of view? Party politics are a sign of the control over all issues wielded by those with the power to frame the discussion. Those with that power are the leaders of culture, which have historically been the wealthiest individuals. In the modern world, this influence is manifested most clearly in control of mass media, through which the society is informed about its choices, and the implications of each choice.

    In the final examination, Rousseau might have been correct to think that a republic could only function on the small scale, because the larger the nations, the more republics are prone to the vices that we notice in them today. In a small republic, with perhaps a population of fifty thousand, everyone can expect to be heard. There would be no excuse for oversimplification, since the infrastructure for communicating ideas at such a small scale would be readily available, and people could demand to be heard without having to pay millions to broadcast their opinions. However, Rousseau was looking at a world between the natural and the technological – communication was still limited by the speeds of beasts of burden and of ships. Today, we have far faster communications, with far more widespread capabilities. Rousseau's other objections notwithstanding, our modern communications media should be able to overcome many of the difficulties building a large Republic would pose. That is in theory – in practice, we face the problem of polarization of opinion and oversimplification.

Time and the Human Condition

This is not to say that there has not been an improvement between our modern mode of government and those of the ancient and medieval world, but that the improvement is less than what it is claimed to be. Party politics, especially if it posits simple dualities, is by definition a vehicle of oversimplification, and therefore is the chief element in the way we govern ourselves that has to be reassessed. If an idea is not considered politically expedient, or a topic has no easy answer, it simply will not get discussed. And we are schooled to accept this. Most people in nations with such a party system cannot conceive of anything else. The fact that this is how we are governed has absolute effects on everything, since all topics in the popular discourse becomes simplified to a duality, and everything the government controls – including incomparable resources – is touched by the decision-making process.

How did party politics come about? Well, most of the founding fathers of the United States were genuinely against party politics. Parties began in an earnest debate concerning the federalism (strong central government and dependent state governments instead of anti-federalism, which is weak central government and independent state governments) embodied in the Constitution, and unfortunately did not diminish after the victor in the debate – the federalists (at that time, the Republicans) – was determined by the Civil War.

France was the originator of the classic political duality during the French Revolution starting in 1789, and the terms "left" and "right" which we use to describe political positions actually refer to where the radical and more moderate factions in opposition sat in the assembly hall during the tumult of the revolution. Revolutions always produce strict dualities because people simply do not have time to sort out subtle positions, and polarization is unavoidable. Incidentally, that government fell apart multiple times, ultimately to Napoleon, but since it had such a massive impact, every detail of it remains important.

Applying Perspective

The British Parliamentary parties, of course, date back to when Parliament was divided into the government, which supported the king's policies, and the opposition, which opposed the government. The duality in parliament was a convenient way for the king to maintain control of the country while giving the nobility and upper yeomanry the right to have some say. The specifics of this arrangement broke down in the English Civil War in the 17th century, but there has been a limited party system in Britain since then to this day. As these three countries spread their influence around the world – Britain and France through imperialism, and America through a variety of means – they spread the seeds of the party system, and ensured it would dominate politics around the world.

To avoid party politics, the only solution any republic has been able to implement has been to multiply the number of parties in the government. With ten or more parties, the discussion becomes far more intellectually complicated, and the points of view of the people can be accurately represented. This is a coalition government, because to make any decision a coalition of many parties has to be built. However, people still need to pay attention to make sure coalitions do not solidify into two or three factions, which would simply duplicate a lesser party system. On each issue, there should be different alignments in the coalitions, otherwise the people are simply being given a duplicate of the left wing – right wing spectrum created in the French Revolution, and in times of trouble there would be solidification of factions.

Would a coalition government with many parties necessarily be more democratic? Compared to a bipolar party system, yes, but there are other roadblocks to the ideal system. The first and most important is the politics of fear. Fear in general is in large part due to lack of perspective, and though a coalition government can facilitate the broadening of perspective, the consciousness of the individual is still a limit.

The practical effect of fear is to induce people to seek safety, or to encourage them to lash out against the unknown.

This will be examined further in the section on law, but politics is essentially a continuum between greater freedom to the individual, which can be defined as liberalism (this is not the definition in common use, but is closer to the proper use of the term), and greater safety to the society, which will be the definition of conservatism. It is important to note that there is a continuum, and not simply two points of view. And on top of that, each person will be at a different point on the continuum on each issue. A person might be twenty percent liberal on gun control, but fifteen percent conservative on the rights of the accused. It is inconceivable that a person would be on the same side of the spectrum on every issue, much less in the exact same place. The human mind also rarely conceives of anything approaching the extremes on this continuum – most ideas will lie very close to the center.

Those definitions apply to politics. For government, there are a number of different continuums that might be applied, and the most basic is that between democracy and authoritarianism. Ultimate democracy would be approaching anarchy, and will emphasize the defense of individual freedom, and ignore public safety. The ultimate authoritarian government emphasizes safety, and ignores individual freedom. In a monarchy, for instance, the king's primarily responsibility is to defend the land and its fertility, the welfare of his people – both temporal and spiritual, and to ensure the succession so that there can be stability. The nobility, throughout history, challenges any king that fails to fulfill these duties. There isn't even a discussion about individual freedom in such a system. In a way, since the government does not have any codes dealing with freedom, the people might actually have more freedom than might be expected. On the other hand, there can be no expectation that those freedoms will remain in an authoritarian system, while in a democracy the people themselves will overthrow a government that tries to limit their freedom. The key problem with pure democracy, of course, is not really a lack of safety, but rather the potential tyranny of the majority.

Back to the politics of fear, we can see now that encouraging people to consider safety over freedom is a deliberate attempt to make the government more authoritarian. It is far easier to govern people with an authoritarian government than with a democracy, so the leaders of any nation will tend toward that direction if allowed to. Note that there is nothing inherently wrong with an authoritarian government in a vacuum. It all distills down to a basic question: would you rather die than lose your freedom, or would you rather lose your freedom than die? People advocating the former over the latter are few and far between, since despite belief in higher principles, people have difficulty seeing the point of freedom in this world if they are dead.

The problem with the politics of fear is two-fold. First, in most cases where it is employed, the government was founded to be democratic rather than authoritarian, and is moving towards safety through the ignorance of the people instead of their consent. In such a situation, the people will have no chance to moderate the trend, and to keep the authoritarianism from going too far. History is littered with representative governments sliding across with increasing velocity toward the other side, and the new authoritarian government invariably becomes so extreme that it ends up being incapable of actually maintaining the public safety. The Roman Republic/Empire is a classic example. The Roman Republic was founded after the overthrow of the monarchy in the late sixth century to early fifth century B.C., and its army was an elite one called into service only when there was an imminent threat to the republic – in other words, it did not have a standing army. However, at the end of the second century B.C., Marius convinced the Senate and People of Rome that there was a serious threat that required conscription and a standing army. Marius himself acted in good faith, but with the next century, Sulla, Pompey, and then Caesar, would use a combination of fear and control over the military to impose dictatorships. To an extent trusting Marius, the Senate had neglected to consider the ultimate consequence of the use of fear tactics, and as the men after Marius used such tactics and gained influence over the new model army, the Senate was decreasingly able to control the situation. When Augustus finally restored order after a generation of civil wars, he claimed that he had saved the Republic, and that he would require certain powers to continue to defend Rome from its enemies, and thus Rome was introduced to its first emperor – though Augustus took the title of "First Citizen."

The second reason, aside from this unintentional slide into authoritarianism, has already been alluded to: the politics of fear limit perspective and distort the sense of time into a very narrow range by demanding immediate action. Both history and the future are dangerous to governments, since those in power are there because of the status quo, so they attempt to control the nation by focusing the attention of the people on day-to-day conflicts. Keeping people afraid of something specific, ideally something that lacks any deep history, the elusive 'now' becomes the focus of public discourse. Fear demands immediate response, and does not allow for idealism. This is why cold "realism" becomes favored. With all the perceived danger and insecurity, people feel that idealism, which would temporarily destabilize things in favor of a better future, is intolerable and dangerous. Of course, this creation of a realism that opposes idealism suits those in power fine – idealism has an odd way of overthrowing the establishment, or at least demanding serious reforms. The powerful prefer to make token reforms, and these are called "realistic" while measures that would actually solve certain problems are called idealistic.

Realism defines a narrow range of possibilities, and considers only a short range of time. Take the oil crises in the United States, for instance. When people are told oil prices are going up, they immediately seek targets, and officials gladly oblige by offering up foreign oil, clamoring to suggest that drilling more domestically might increase oil reserves and make America less reliant on foreign oil. This, of course, is a short-term solution. It totally ignores the fact that, in a hundred years at most, there will be no more easily accessible oil, and our current usage will be untenable. A hundred years is not a long time in history. Some people alive today will live to see the forced end of oil reliance. For those who have not carefully considered the situation, it is easy to say that we will simply turn to alternative fuel sources when the time comes, but that is only because we have been conditioned to think through things on a day-to-day level rather than with true perspective. What will happen, for instance, to aircraft? Perhaps we can put fuel cells and batteries into cars, but try flying with those alternatives. We will have some fuel held back for flights, and we will be able to synthesize limited amounts, but without some better ideas, traveling by air will suddenly become very expensive for the average person.

This, and many other very obvious issues looming ahead of us, is not even discussed in the public forum. In fact, the deterioration of the environment is not really discussed either. At least, it is not at a coherent level. So there can be no expectation that people will take the environment into account when voting for their leaders, since they have no way of telling which policies will strike the correct balance. When there is lack of discussion on a topic, and fear has induced the public to seek greater safety, the voters will inevitably shy away from politicians that take an idealistic stance, or any position requiring innovation.

Time and the Human Condition

The clearest sense that party politics and the politics of fear distort time can be seen in the media. In ancient times, of course, there would be other signs, but because the media is meant to serve as a window into the political process in the modern day, it can provide immediately apparent indications of trends. How confined is the sense of time on television? Consider the "soundbite". This is a very recent phenomenon that developed because politics ceased to be a thorough discussion with intelligent examination of the issues, and started being a process of appealing to emotions like fear. If politics was expected to deal with the issues thoroughly, the devolution of the discussion into "soundbites" would not be tolerated. Instead, politicians have stopped giving speeches, and have started giving lists of "soundbites". Many of our leaders are actually incapable of stating a coherent position without help from a retinue of aids. However, since the public is ready to accept "soundbites" – in fact eager to, since the packaged words allow us to be intellectually lazy – there is no longer any need to explain positions. Politicians can just throw in catchwords meant to elicit emotions, and their words will be guaranteed airtime. If they actually try to explain their platforms in detail, in a dry but logical way, their speech will never reach cable, much less broadcasting.

This is a fairly critical picture of the way we govern ourselves today. It is to some extent meant as an antidote to the way we have been congratulating ourselves for our progress, and failing to take further steps in the right direction. For the past century, Britain and America in particular have talked about the spread of democracy and the defense of democracy, while failing to develop, or even to maintain an understanding, how their own systems worked. Our governments are not perfect, so we should not allow our thirst for something better to stagnate on the premise that these governments are the best humankind can manage. As for the spread of such systems, the democratic nations of the world need to remember that government is by consent of the people, not by consent of world opinion. Democratic values have to develop from the inside, otherwise they will never be respected, and always seen as something foreign. By being critical, we can develop discussions about the flawed areas in our system that fail to get discussed, and also about the way we might safely introduce our ideas and open up a dialogue with non-democratic nations, all of which are completely and conveniently ignored by the system of public discourse we have today.

Is the state of things entirely the fault of politicians or those in power? Not at all. As with so many other things, it is a feedback loop. In this case, it is a loop between government, education, the continuum between liberty and security, ideas of progress, and the dominant visual culture. In other words, virtually everything described so far comes into play. Government is at such an all encompassing level – determining the course of entire countries – it is naturally affected by everything that happens to be occurring. While everyone in a nation might not be equally responsible for the condition of that nation's government, everyone shares a part in the responsibility, however small. And that is regardless of whether the government allows participation or not.

Time and the Human Condition

On Law, Justice, and Order

There are two types of laws – those that grant freedom to do certain things, and those that give people freedom from certain things. Laws in the first group are often called "rights" or "freedoms" while the second group is often called merely "law," because almost all laws are of the second type. Society was originally built for mutual security, so it should not come as a surprise that its laws reflect that. The way governments trended toward oligarchy and monarchy first before turning towards democracy and the republic is also a reflection of it. Over time, a society will move towards one or the other of these two poles in the continuum of laws. In the times when laws instilling greater freedoms to the individual are favored, the society as a whole can be said to be tending towards liberalism, and while the impulse towards safety shows a trend to conservatism.

The coupling of law and order is an oversimplification of what is really a spectrum with lawlessness on the one hand, complete order on the other, and justice in the middle, the mean between the two extremes. This spectrum is precisely analogous to the continuum between freedom to and freedom from, so that lawlessness represents complete freedom, while pure order is also complete safety. In all situations, barring those times in war when the courthouse itself is under threat of being bombed, the correct coupling – essential to the proper running of a society – is law and justice. Otherwise the emphasis would be on one or the other of the extremes, rather than on balance.

Applying Perspective

Usually, the side of the spectrum that gains more importance over time is that favoring order and safety. This practical distinction between justice, as a search for balance, and order, as a search for safety, mainly centers on how police pursue a case and whether the normal processes of law are followed. The established processes of law are the rules agreed upon by the society as a whole, and people rightfully expect the treatment 'justice' implies. Only in times of intense fear and insecurity so people value order over justice, and support the harsher measures that 'order' implies – these harsher measures being anything the society as a whole recognizes as unusual and extralegal. In the United States, for instance, the standards of justice are established by the Bill of Rights and by court precedent. If in certain cases the protections of the Bill of Rights are refused, or if a court outlines special circumstances where the previous precedent no longer applies, then order is being valued over justice. This should not be confused with the natural evolution of justice to resolve faults that existed before. The changes based on order rather than justice are always in response to tensions or fear, and always limit the freedom of individuals.

As already noted, despite the fact that we have no logical reason to be, we live in a time of fear and insecurity. Party politics encourages the use of fear as a means to maintain power and the status quo. We have lived in this political environment since the end of the Second World War. The result of valuing order over justice has been quite clear since the United States from the anti-communist hearings of the fifties and the use of police force against peaceful protests – both in the Civil Rights movement and the early Peace movement – in the sixties. The new laws designed to keep order are piling up irrespective of justice, and show no sign of diminishing.

Time and the Human Condition

We know what order looks like, in all its strict sterility, but what is justice? The problem with finding a balance is that the matter is, by definition, subjective. Justice is called blind because it is not supposed to base subjective judgments on the nature of the defendant and a judge should limit the effect of his own personal feelings, not because the merits of the case should not be taken into account. It is accepted that the punishment needs to fit the crime, and getting the proper measure and balance is a subjective matter. It can only be objective if there is no attempt to make the fit, and instead a blanket punishment is set for every instance of a certain type of crime. That is the reason why order is preferred in dire times – since it is straightforward and relatively unambiguous, and requires none of the time and effort that the full justice system requires. In dire times, there is simply a lack of the time necessary to carry cases through the entire justice. As might be expected, the ability to decide what is just, in light of the enlightened subjectivity it involves, requires deep perspective – in fact, ultimate justice requires infinite perspective – extensive knowledge of moral dilemmas, and of changes in theory over time. But there are practical theories that can be applied, and people can actually readily analyze laws without recourse to higher levels of consciousness.

Let's begin with the lowest requirement. Law, being developed to mediate relations between humans, should not limit a person's activities in private life unless it can be shown to directly affect another human being in an adverse manner. Since it is the basis for law in the first place, it should be able to withstand any criticism. With that guideline in place, we can take a look at the ways people can react to a law, and use that to see whether a law is just. There are three ways people can react to a law. Either they would not have committed the transgression whether there was a law against it or not, or they would have committed the transgression, but are deterred

Applying Perspective

by the law and the associated penalty, or they will commit the transgression regardless of the law. We can now make profiles of laws. In reaction to laws against murder, for instance, the great majority of people are in the first group, far less people are in the second group, and the third can be less or equal to the second group, but not more if a law can be said to have any real affect. Over time, the profile of a particular law will change, and deviate from the intended profile. The more important the law, the more reform will be necessary as it deviates, even slightly, from the ideal profile. All law codes can be judged by their homicide code, and if the society has a disproportionate number of people committing murder despite the law, even if most people who would commit murder are still deterred by the law, then something is wrong either with the code or the culture. More often it is the culture, so that changes in the law might have no effect at all.

Traffic laws will show a marked contrast to homicide laws. Reacting to the speed limit, a healthy percentage of the population will be in the first group, far fewer in the second, and the great majority of people will be in the third. The speed limit might best be considered a courtesy law – encouraging people to think of others while driving. Such laws actually end up serving more to provide revenue to the state than to actually deter people. Unfortunately, when courtesy laws are lumped with more serious laws, and enforced by the same officers, those more serious laws are treated with the same abandon. Drunk driving laws are traffic laws, but far more serious than the speed limit. Most people are part of the first group as far as drunk driving goes, but entirely too many are part of the third. The reason for this is that, subconsciously, they have associated all traffic laws together. They certainly don't think of drunk driving as potential homicide.

With these profiles, we can make a few generalizations. First, if in a certain society, a law has a different profile for one race or class of person than another, then that law has to be recognized as having a disproportionate impact. It may have been designed to have such an impact, and perhaps for a good reason, or perhaps the imbalance lies in enforcement. Perhaps the law simply says to obey the speed limit, but in a certain area the speed limit is impossibly low, or not displayed properly, then it is the fault of law. If, on the other hand, police patrols are organized such that certain areas are covered more heavily than others, and these areas somehow produce more traffic violations and other crimes, then clearly enforcement is at issue. It should be noted that justice cannot assume genetic predispositions or any of the other assumptions thrown around in less tolerant times. Justice is also not preemptive – that is what order is for. Only order can be preemptive, which is why it is used in urgent times. No one will object to preventing murder, if by the standards of laws against attempted murder it can be proved that a murder was about to be committed, but few other crimes require the urgency that stern order and preemptive prevention brings. Certainly, preemptively arresting people for theft would be highly irregular, and in almost all systems the authorities wait for the crime to be committed, before they trap the criminals.

Now we come to the tough part of justice: the moral dilemmas. There is one rule that all justice systems, if they make any claim of being just, should abide by – every case must be decided on its own merits, with conscience and previous precedent taken into consideration. Moral dilemmas are the reason why this rule must be followed. A famous dilemma is the situation in which a poor man needs medicine to save his wife's life, but clearly lacks the money to purchase the medicine, and has tried every recourse short of stealing it. Is he justified in stealing it? If there was a blanket theft law, with a single punishment that might be based on precedent (since every previous theft case would have resulted in the same punishment) but fails to consider the merits of the case and conscience, that would not be justice. In the case of this dilemma, it is clear that the man, if he commits the theft, should be punished, but not nearly to the extent other thieves would be. The circumstances dictate that the man's actions were partially justified, and cannot be reasonably blamed for his choice. His actions did not significantly harm society. Some judges, in certain cases, are compelled to "make an example" of someone by giving a heavier sentence than justice would demand. Such an act violates this rule of justice, because the case has to be judged solely in a vacuum, and not in relation to the possible acts of future criminals.

So the punishment is key in deciding whether justice is done. If in a society, a particular race or class is given a disproportionate punishment for a similar crime, that punishment was unjust. I sincerely hope this isn't a revelation, but I know it isn't practiced. That is why law has to be discussed, and perspective applied to it, because the reality is so far away from being reasonable or just that only lack of empathy allows people to tolerate it. The main reason why law and the understanding of it is so vital can be seen whenever a person's freedom is limited, ostensibly to protect another. If authority crosses the line, and begins to apply the order model instead of the justice model, the net effect will be to prosecute any deviations from the norm, with steadily increasing vigilance. After all, order is ultimately uniformity, while justice is something quite different.

Law has deep effects, and can scar history itself. When African-Americans in the United States speak of injustices done to them, those injustices are enshrined in law – from laws protecting slavery to the Jim Crow laws and segregation. Law is easily and often used by the powerful to gain an added advantage over the weak, so it is necessary for all those that have the fortune of living under a representative government to notice such injustice and speak out against it. That, in the United States, the majority eventually heeded the oppressed minority is a testament, albeit a bit delayed, to the leaps of justice humanity is capable of. We must not think that we have reached the summit. There are further leaps to be made, and, lacking some higher level of consciousness, we will always have more room to develop our sense of justice.

Applying Perspective

On Reality, Fantasy, and Vicarious Experience

I have noted that fear of both the past and the future often paralyzes people. In many cases, this intellectual paralysis occurs right in front of the television set. This criticism should come as no surprise – we have only the moment between the past and the future in which we can affect change, and most people use this time in the most ludicrous and ironic of ways. The reason I take on this topic here, though, is because the vicarious experience through television often has a distinct affect on people's perception of events, especially through the news and documentaries. This affect is primarily due to the shift from written culture to visual culture – otherwise people would rely more on the newspaper or books for their perceptions, and have adequate time to process the information, distilling it into understanding. The speed allowed by visual culture may be more able to transmit the vast amounts information available today than the written media, but that information is useless, or even counterproductive, without understanding.

The problems of television are the problems of visual culture. It is basically neutral – producing no benefit, but not doing any harm – except for when people use it to think for them. Visual culture conveys emotions easier than it conveys ideas, and ideas faster than it can explain them. It is no fault of those involved in the news media themselves, but rather comes from a combination of the traits of visual culture. A picture, like a song, inspires emotion first, through the colors, textures, and the actual subject matter of the piece. Only after that does it inspire vague ideas, and only art aficionados end up attempting to analyze art deeply. With television, this nature of the visual component is coupled with the full affect of music as well – which is placed subtly in the background, but has its effect. During news segments dealing with war, for instance, the music is distinctly militant, inspiring very particular feelings. Therefore, when people rely on their television for explanations, commentary, and analysis, they first get irrational emotions, then scattered ideas, both of which outgun rational argument.

The basic affects of visual culture are further made problematic by the way television news is presented almost instantaneously twenty-four hours a day. This means that it will only reflect the most immediate reactions people tend to have toward any event. And, naturally, the first reaction is always an emotional one. No matter what news it is, the first reaction is the gut reaction, which establishes how we feel about it. Most of the news is composed of these immediate snapshots bereft of any real thought. Often, guest 'experts,' most of them groomed for their media roles, are available to provide a quick analysis. This analysis is inevitably pedestrian, and driven by emotions – usually leading to shouting matches which make the news more entertaining, boosting viewer ratings. No one knowledgeable who wishes to provide an honest analysis would be willing to comment on major political, economic, or social issues without extensive time to consider the matter free from initial impressions.

So the issues created by the visual medium itself are compounded by the speed with which the news is released. And any real analysis is drowned out by the constant flow of fresh news. Dry analysis, after all, is not nearly as exciting as breaking news, live scoops, and the spot analysts shouting at each other, which means it doesn't get the ratings, won't attract advertising, and so cannot be shown. That is the nature of television as a medium today. No one involved is necessarily to blame. If anyone is to blame for the impact this medium has, it is the viewers who are beset by mental laziness, which the education system likely introduced them to, and do not seek information from other sources – sources that take some more time before reaching a judgment on an issue, which will help a person on the road to understanding.

All vicarious experience can be taken in the same light, with the same caveat. Taking this back to physics, while the affects of an event can reach you at the speed of light, and information can theoretically reach you at the speed of light, understanding is limited by the speed and depth with which you can think through the situation. Until a person has gained understanding of an event, that event is, in their minds, a vicarious experience – even if they personally went through it. That's a bit complicated, but we have all been in a situation where everything occurring seems to be a dream, and we say that we need some time to process the situation. That is, in fact, exactly what we need. Once the event has been processed, it becomes experience.

The power of the experience derived from an event is inversely proportional to the distance from the event a person was when the information and understanding reached them. Allow me to use a coarse example to clear this up a bit. Consider the assassination of John F. Kennedy. It should be obvious to everyone that John F. Kennedy was not the only one to be affected by it, or to gain experience from it. Everyone in the world who was aware of the event was affected by it, and everyone took some time to process it. For those who reached some understanding, or derived some reasonable conclusion from the tragedy, experience was gained. Many, for instance, felt an increase in personal dedication to the ideals Kennedy expressed, and in the wake of his assassination, the government was able to take important steps in Civil Rights and in the Elimination of Poverty, often explicitly in Kennedy's honor. The power of the potential experience decreased as distance to the event increased, so that while the assassination of Kennedy could inspire great works in America, where his death had central significance, that sort of legislative change could not be expected anywhere else, though individuals around the world were powerfully troubled by Kennedy's fate.

Until information is processed, and becomes understanding, it remains vicarious experience, regardless of whether a person was involved in the event or not. So, even if we did not take part in an event, we can gain some limited experience – far less than those actually involved – by processing information and seeing if we can derive some new knowledge from it. The problem with vicarious experience delivered by television is that the medium actually discourages thought, and the processing of information, by bombarding the viewer with images and raw information.

Can someone else's analysis ever be enough to give a person any sort of understanding of an event? From the discussion above, it should be clear that gaining understanding is purely an internal process, and so the most another person can do is help you along the road to understanding, perhaps by pointing you in the right direction. The criticism of television, then, is that it leave people adrift in information, and before allowing them to reach understanding, throws more information into the mess. But, the burden of thought is always on the individual.

So, the full process is as follows. Before something happens, anyone considering it is pondering fantasy – so that science-fiction writers might actually predict an event that will happen in the future, but for them it is purely a fantasy, and their interaction with it remains at the level of speculation. Then an event happens in reality, and has its own infinitesimal

Applying Perspective

"now." As the light from the event is able to reach people, they start being affected by it, such that those closest to the event are affected first. Then information about the event is released through various media, each traveling at different speeds. Those who can actually see the event receive information when their brains sort out the sensory receptions. Some might also feel it, hear it, or smell it, but the rest of us get information through the news, through word of mouth, or by other means. In every case, this is still raw information and constitutes vicarious experience. This is not what most people mean when they say vicarious experience, but the practical affect of being removed from an event is present in everyone before they can process it. Besides, since the event actually affects everyone, regardless of how minor that effect might be, the line drawn by the meaning of "vicarious" used commonly makes no sense. The term only makes sense to explain the gap between having information and having experience. And experience can only be attained when a person distills and transforms the information into something meaningful. So, ultimately time is necessary to convert vicarious experience into actual experience. Without time to gain understanding, true knowledge is impossible. All perspective therefore depends on time taken to develop knowledge about a situation, because without that time, the perspective is vacuous.

Part 5
Human Understanding

Human Understanding

Sensation and Reflection - How Perspective is Built Over Time

Attempting to gain knowledge of human understanding, John Locke developed theories based on the idea that all human knowledge is derived from our experiences. However, unlike his predecessors who thought along this line, Locke divided experience into two components: sensation and reflection. Sensation is input from the senses, and is the fundamental basis of knowledge, while reflection is the application of thought processes on that sensory input, which ranges from making comparisons and associations between inputs to deriving conclusions and applying them to other sensations. Since Locke wrote at the end of the seventeenth century, there has been a great deal of development in philosophy, and the entire creation of the discipline of psychology, but the pairing of sensation and reflection is a useful tool for understanding thought. It is essential, in fact, because Locke's theories on human understanding are the basis on which he built his political philosophy. Even though philosophers like Kant may have developed better understanding of epistemology, our politics are still very much indebted to the philosophers of the seventeenth and eighteenth century.

    Locke's arguments assumes philosophical realism – that there is a real universe independent of our thoughts – and the discussion that follows will discuss knowledge and experience as if there is a universe we interact with that is not idealistic. If there is no universe independent of thought, then our experiences in the universe are actually shaped by our thoughts.

So, knowledge would not be derived from experience, but rather our knowledge would determine our experiences. For Locke's arguments to be valid, this cannot be, and there has to be a universe that will in some way inform us.

We can use Locke's conception of understanding to construct the way perspective is built over time. While much has been made of the levels of perspective and how they are related to different spans of time, and of the application of perspective, very little has been said about the internal workings of perspective. All perspective has its heart in knowledge, so in all cases the beginning can be seen through sensation and reflection.

The first level of perspective is individual experience. However, as I have defined this, it is comprised not only of a single person's experience, but also the experiences of others who have communicated directly with the person. The reason the two have been combined is due to the fact that they share the same bounds of time – both a person's experiences and his or her communications with others are limited by that person's lifetime. Limits in space can also be considered at this point. Because the only sense that typically operates at the speed of light is sight, and because communication until recently has been limited to speeds far slower than light, those inputs that a person can process are severely limited by that person's position in space, and not only the span of the person's life. Therefore, though a person's experience has been expanded only moderately through modern technology, it has much more dramatic on perspective. Since the perspective level includes information derived from communication with others, the modern modes of communication have created a massive increase in information to process.

While the construction of individual experience is fairly simple, culture is far more complex, even more so than historical and eternal knowledge. As noted before, culture's primary function is to mediate, particularly in dense communities where conflict between world-views can frequently arise. No effort is required to develop a culture – it seems to form naturally, and for this reason humans are considered natural community builders. To some extent, since the community is living in the same space at the same time, it might be expected that a set of common experiences can be found. But culture is more than common experiences and their attendant perspectives. It is perpetuated through times for which certain experiences have long been alien, though it makes occasional concessions in order to remain relevant. Let's take a look at some of the common elements of culture in order to get a better sense of how it gives a person certain perspectives, and what knowledge those perspectives are based on.

The most dominant and persistent area of culture is usually aesthetics, which is directly related to sensation. The way things should look is determined initially by some consensus of experience between people about what is pleasing to the eye, from clothing to art to furniture, and subsequently determined by precedent. The established way things should look eventually becomes the only way people within a certain culture have ever experienced, and all other models of visual aesthetics will seem alien and therefore less preferable.

Hearing works the same way. The Western model of music is substantially different from the Chinese model, for instance. Western music, based on the model of classical music starting in the sixteenth and seventeenth century, spread through Europe because of the common Christian touchstone. Nevertheless, despite a common religion and a great deal of cultural norms associated with that religion, each region in Europe developed its own versions of Western music, such that the Italian style is distinctive from the German, which is in turn clearly different from the Russian. The popularity of the music from different regions changes through time because from 1500 to 1900, Europe was in the midst of cultural tumult after a millennium of stability. With all these specific differences, any form of Western music is still identifiably different from traditional Chinese music, and anyone groomed on one will have some difficulty appreciating the other, while a change of music within each system will take much less time to get accustomed to.

Taste and smell are both functions of cuisine, which may be the most commonly shared element of culture. Clearly, culture determines those elements of sensation that relate to aesthetics, until a new aesthetic trend seeks to overturn the dictates of the old culture. Like these codes of aesthetics, other cultural norms start with general preference at an early time, and are solidified through time, only to be struck down or changed as the dissent to a particular norm gains sway.

Cultural perspective, then, begins with group preference, and continues through the constant reinforcement of the precedent. Group preference does not require communication between individuals – television viewers express their preference by boosting a show's ratings, and similarly there have always been ways to gauge, quite quickly, the popularity of things. Also, it is important to note that only the powerful need to be consulted. The elite determine the cultural standards of art, music, and writing, as well as the other norms. The determination is arrived at through the experiences of the people in relation to the aesthetics, or to the norms. Culture, then, can be properly considered the collected experience of a group of people, from which is synthesized certain preferences that persist over time, until they finally become irrelevant and need to be replaced. Until it is revised, then, a culture can limit what knowledge a person can gain by continuing standards set generations before, and by this limit ensure that a person will definitely have certain sensations, modes of reflection, and a certain set of common knowledge with his or her neighbor. Also, since culture is a matter of precedent, it can be used as a tool to look into the future, because the next generation and perhaps generations after will continue to hold to many of the values and norms of the culture.

Next, let us take a look at how historical perspective is constructed. In all cases, history relies on artifacts from the past – whether these artifacts are archaeological ruins, utensils, art, or written documents. In other words, the construction of historical knowledge is based on the products of the individual knowledge and the cultural norms of people in the past. That is what history examines. In making this examination, history is able to see cultural values that existed before the current culture, and can see more of the variation through space and time. History is not experience, but it examines the experience and knowledge of people to see what effects the past may have on the present, and what assumptions of the present are in fact incorrect. In every culture, people assume that their way is natural and proper, and things cannot be done any other way. Historical perspective does away with this illusion by maintaining a living record of ideas, values, and norms that have lost their immediate relevance, but may be valuable for comparison in times of change.

But how is eternal perspective built? It requires neither historical nor cultural perspective for its conclusions. Science still employs individual knowledge while enhancing it through the use of tools for measurement and an intense application of reflection based on the sensory inputs from those measurements. As noted in the section on quantum mechanics, however, such measurement has its limits, and in many cases thought experiments result in theories before real experiments can confirm the theories and move them into the realm of knowledge about the eternal.

Time and the Human Condition

It might be difficult to grasp the broad spectrum of knowledge about the eternal, so perhaps a definition is in order. Knowledge about the eternal is simply all knowledge that extends for all time. While many conclusions of geology and biology add to eternal perspective, it would be a stretch to consider most of them eternal knowledge. However, those conclusions that concern the fundamental way all planets, or all life, functions, are indeed examples of eternal knowledge. The law of gravitation is eternal knowledge because, even if it requires refinement, it describes how the universe has functioned from as close to the start as possible and predicts how things will work until the end of time, if there is one. Gravity was discovered through personal knowledge, of course, but the manner in which the knowledge can be universally applied makes it knowledge of this level. All knowledge of eternity contributed by science ultimately requires individual experience through measurement and experimentation, otherwise it would violate the philosophy and beliefs of science.

For spirituality, the matter of knowledge and perspective is more complicated. While before the modern era, spiritual belief was considered knowledge, in light of science this has since been amended. Science, through men like Francis Bacon and John Locke, has defined knowledge and logic carefully, and though initially the Enlightenment theorists used this redefinition to try to prove the existence of God, they instead ensured that spirituality would be a matter solely of faith, unsupportable by reason.

This transition begins with the struggle between the inductive reasoning of Bacon and the deductive reasoning of Descartes. Inductive reasoning emphasizes knowledge gained from the senses and experimentation, claiming that only through such experience can knowledge be gained. Deductive reason involves thought experiments – beginning with a solid premise and through thought alone deriving conclusions from the premise. Descartes uses his reasoning to, in his view, prove the existence of God. Locke, building on Bacon's inductive reasoning through his emphasis on sensation and reflection, also applied his method as a defender of reason's ability to prove God's presence, though he rebuked Descartes for some of the earlier philosopher's assumptions about thought. Thanks to these two theorists, people became increasingly confident that reason was not only compatible with the presence of God, but supported spirituality.

Then came Pierre Bayle. Bayle was a profoundly devout man disturbed by this attempt of reason to try and explain God. In dissent, Bayle writes on the exclusiveness of reason and the divine, showing in fact that faith alone can lead to knowledge of God, and that reason was a representation of human arrogance. His argument was powerful, but his intention was to emphasize faith and diminish reason. Unfortunately, through the achievements of men like Newton, reason had gained favor, and Bayle's arguments had the affect of simply turning people away from spiritual explanations for phenomena. The pious Bayle would be remembered as a critic not of reason, but of religion. Incidentally, while arguments through pure logic and reason would rarely be used to prove God after the seventeenth century, the orderly nature of the universe – with gravity ultimately expressed by an elegant equation and many other phenomena seeming absurdly simple once revealed – continues to be used as an indication of the deity's existence.

For centuries, faith has been associated with spirituality while knowledge and reason has been left to science. The response to the conclusions of the Enlightenment was a turn away from organized religion, but this was as much due to the constant religious wars throughout Europe and the intractability of the church hierarchies as to the accomplishments of science. This opened the possibility for forms of spirituality outside the churches, and led to greater emphasis on religious toleration. Voltaire's insistence on religious toleration were a direct result of Bayle's argument that God could not be known through reason – since that point of view logically means that no one person can claim more knowledge of divine truth than another. That spirituality is not compatible with existing notions of knowledge also poses no problem. It agrees with the view that the divine realm would have to exist outside the universe, as discussed in earlier sections, and that consciousness would have to expand before understanding of the divine could be possible.

In a way, it is as if we require a telescope, or a microscope to sharpen our senses so that we can sense things not normally within the realm of human experience. But instead of the tools of science, what we really need to gain knowledge of the spiritual realm is a consciousness that would redefine knowledge from the sensation-reflection coupling to something that does not require interaction with the matter in this universe or thought bounded by the perspectives allowed within this universe. The spiritual area of eternal perspective is built out of different beliefs, faiths, and ideas about the divine. That is all it can be made up of, because actual knowledge of the divine would transcend eternity – transcend time altogether instead of simply stretching from the beginning of time to the end of time. Therefore, actual spiritual knowledge requires a level of perspective beyond the four that are currently possible for human consciousness.

So we have an account of the development of various perspectives in terms of knowledge. Granted, this is only an outline of what might otherwise be a very complicated issue, but it shows perspectives interact or do not interact, and some of the limitations of human perception.

Human Understanding

Time and Stress

Our perception of time colors everything we do. The clearest way to see its effect is to note how our psychology has changed since industrialization in the late nineteenth century brought a new fragmentation of the perception of time. Until the industrial era, time was natural. The segmentation of time into days has a physical precedence – the rotation of Earth around its axis. Waking up at dawn, setting appointments based on mealtimes and noon, and finishing up the day at sunset, is all natural. While the hour can be divided based on the position of the sun during the day, minutes and seconds are completely artificial – a fact that is often forgotten in the modern world. It is also no coincidence that, by the natural timekeeping, we will get less work done in the winter because our days will be shorter, since that is also time we would normally have to conserve energy and food. This association between our behavior and our environment is the product of millions of years of conditioning, so it should come as no surprise that altering this order drastically within a hundred years would cause us a great deal of stress. So, let us examine the reasons behind the change, its manifestations, and its further effects.

First, though, the nature of stress itself should be outlined. In a purely physical sense, stress is a force that strains or deforms a body. That's a good way to conceive of stress in general. In terms of this discussion, human stress has two components – physical stress on the body and mental stress. We will be focusing on mental stress. The specific symptoms vary from person to person, but the major events that cause the greatest stress for people are more or less uniform. Getting fired from a job, the death of a loved one, or a divorce, are all examples of major stressors. Minor stressors are literally any trouble that comes around – work, bills to pay, arrangements that need to be made, and lack of sleep. While humans can naturally deal with a certain amount of such stressors, there is always a point where the frequency and magnitude of stressors begin to take their toll.

Some people claim to prefer an environment of constant stress – its highly touted in the business world that such an environment is more productive. Of course, for the short term this is true since the high level of stress is caused by a quantity of work that is nearly impossible for the individual to manage. Very quickly, however, the mental affects become apparent, and the pace of work and stress becomes unsustainable. The examination that follows will deal specifically with how the conception of time interacts with stress, how the modern era of stress was created by a drive for productivity, and the negative affects of modern stress on our ability to understand and develop perspective.

In Christian belief, there has long been the idea that nature in general is base and fundamentally corrupting, and we must tame and transcend our own natures. However, contrary to what might initially be expected, this did not inspire the reinvention of time. The change was initialized by respect for nature, not disdain for it. The Age of Enlightenment in the seventeenth and eighteenth century attacked the pessimistic view of nature presented by the Christian church, suggesting that we could actually know a great deal about nature, that it was orderly and sensible instead of frightening, and that this order was clearly the mark of God. The major spiritual contention of the Enlightenment philosophers was that we could get a sense of the divine from the creation itself – because, after all, why would a perfect deity create nature to be shunned?

It was the approach of these philosophers that led them to fully develop a new sense of time. Their approach for studying nature and the universe was either inductive or deductive, and inductive study would become dominant with the achievements of Isaac Newton. This was called natural philosophy at the time, as it had been in Aristotle's day, but would eventually be known as science. Science examines the universe through observation and measurement, the formation of hypotheses based on those notes, and the use of experimentation or logical proofs to prove or disprove the hypotheses. The key here is measurement, since physics requires the precise measurement of time. Our basic system and words for time – hours, minutes, and seconds – may have had precedence before the seventeenth and eighteenth century, but those concepts had only casual relevance. It was Huygens, the famous physicist, who invented the pendulum clock in 1657, after examining carefully the physics of the pendulum.

So the clock was, from the start, an invention by and for natural philosophers, though it would also be quickly applied to navigation. For a long time, it remained only in use for specific purposes. Even if small, affordable clocks had been available, it would have been unusual for people to purchase them for anything beyond novelty. Rural life requires a very particular sense of the passing of the seasons and weather patterns, but a more precise sense of time is unnecessary. On the weekends, farmers in Europe would head into town for market days and church. How do you know when to head to church? The bell tolls, of course. For town dwellers like artisans and merchants, time also continued to flow naturally. So while the clock was used to discover nature, it was not meant to constrain nature in any way. It became a symbol, though, of the rational and explainable working of the universe, and its internal workings were a metaphor for the interrelationship of everything in the universe. Eventually, people would begin to describe the universe as a machine, and the symbol for that machine has most often been the clock.

The real catalyst for the change in the average person's understanding of the flow of time was industrialization, when machines began dominating people. In the early textile industry, from the mid to late nineteenth century, the engine that drove the production line was set to a speed, and everyone in the factory had to work at that pace. Early textile towns usually revolved around the factory, so keeping work times was not an issue. But, as industries grew, it quickly became natural for workdays to be established, and for these to be moderated by clocks – yet another machine that would drive the workers. From the beginning of industry to the start of the twentieth century, machines were firmly considered more important than workers, and laborers actively protested the way they were treated. Prevented by law from unionizing, their protests were often put down violently by the authorities. Perhaps the most famous clash was the Haymarket protest, riot, and trial, which started on May 1, 1886 and resonated for decades to come. May Day continues to have significance for unions, socialists, and groups supporting worker's rights.

The labor question was the most dominant domestic issue both in the United States and in Europe during most of the growth of industry. While the principal goal of the labor movements was to establish a forty-hour limit to the workweek, the concern about the subordination of man to machine was very clear. It was even embodied in movies, including the silent film *Metropolis*, which shows a future extrapolated from the trends of the time, and Charlie Chaplin's *Modern Times*, which included a famous assembly line gag routine in which Chaplin was having trouble keeping up with the machine. Thanks to the efforts of labor, the forty-hour week was eventually granted, but the net result was to encourage even tighter timekeeping methods by company managers. At the start of the twentieth century, Frederick Winslow Taylor published *The Principles of Scientific Management* that, among other suggestions, demanded a regimentation of production using time studies, which would actually clock the motions of workers to find optimum speeds for efficiency. His suggestions would gain increasing attention through the labor troubles and the concessions of business, and workers would be tied even closer to machines.

    So, why are workers no longer concerned about the domination of machines? It is still an underlying current in society, and one that appears in movies frequently in the form of man-against-machine struggles. But, instead of reclaiming a natural sense of time, we exalt ourselves with atomic clocks. The first step in the mass acceptance of machined time was the product of the Ford assembly lines – the cheap automobile. Starting in the twenties, machines were no longer solely under the control of corporations, and a middle class of car owners was born. The car became a symbol of the American dream, and people began to take pride in these machines, assigning to them value that the mere function of transportation could not account for. It was only the first of a whole host of machines that people would soon be able to own, and the more control people had over machines, the more natural the new sense of time felt. From the time it takes to get from one place to another, to the time it takes to communicate, to cooking times, to radio and television programming times, to school schedules, and finally to becoming impatient after ten seconds when an internet webpage is taking too long to load, we have very quickly developed a new relationship to time.

    That is a brief history of how we went from sundial time to watch time, and it will help us to see modern manifestations of how the finer measurement of time affects us. To start with an example simple yet telling, Daylight Savings Time provides an excellent case study. While many places around the world do not observe it, most industrialized countries do set the clocks forward in the spring and back in autumn. That this practice was first proposed in 1907 should not be surprising in light of the history outlined above. And, predictably, the reason was to boost productivity by making full use of the daylight hours in the summer time. It was first put into use in Germany in 1916, during the First World War when that country needed the productivity, and the United States followed in 1918 shortly after entering the war. The practice ended at the end of the war, was revived in the Second World War, but was again stopped until 1966, when it was proposed instead for the conservation of energy.

Daylight Savings Time, a minor change in our now rigid measurement of time that occurs twice a year, has serious effects on individuals for a short period after the change. The obvious immediate affect is a disruption of sleeping patterns, but this in turn causes irritation and accidents. After Daylight Savings Time takes affect, there is usually a brief spike in car accidents. In general, the disorientation causes stress of varying degrees. Such an arbitrary change would be meaningless if we were not first tied to a very precise sense of time, and accustomed to the passing of every minute, so that the passing of sixty causes a noticeable difference in our behavior. Predictably, Daylight Savings Time is unpopular among farmers and others working with animals, since the animals continue on their regular schedule irrespective of the clocks, and though it might seem at first to be a minor difference, our extremely fractional sense of time makes the effect far more extreme that it needs to be.

The real power of watch time is far more wide ranging, and has changed our behavior most seriously in our patience and our ability to delay gratification. For a person who cannot have constant contact with clocks, it is impossible to be fifteen minutes late. A person might actually be late, but it would be difficult for anyone to be legitimately aggravated by someone being late by less than an hour. The kind of aggravation we feel while in heavy traffic for half an hour would be nonsense to people accustomed to making hundred mile journeys on foot, which was indeed the kind of walking range people expected of themselves before travel by sea became affordable and safe in the eighteenth century. Similarly, our ability to wait is affected by the way we divide time, and the fact that we can count the minutes passing by in the way we might have counted the days centuries ago.

We are not so much aware of the passing of the continuum of time as we are the passing of units of time. It is often said that time seems to pass faster when one is having fun, and passes slower in times of boredom or frustration. The reason for this perception is simple – when a person is occupied with something that captures the attention, the person is less likely to think about the passing of time. Meanwhile, when bored or otherwise waiting to get out of a situation like school or work, a person might literally stare at a clock noting the passing of the seconds. The same idea is behind the saying that a watched pot never boils – it is not necessary for us to actually have a clock in front of us to measure the passing of tiny fractions of time, but rather we need only to have the concept of seconds and minutes in our minds and to be conditioned to consider the time spent in such terms. If not from day-to-day interaction with the culture, this conditioning occurs in schools, as students grow accustomed to very precise and completely artificial schedules, and from television, as kids anticipate the time of their favorite program. While time itself is a continuum, and we move through it in that way, we perceive it in chunks, and if we are conditioned to think that there are more chunks in a given amount of actual time, then it will seem to us that there is actually more time, and we plan to do more accordingly.

We are also conditioned to be impatient. In a trend that has built up over the past century, as every new generation outpaces the older one, the machination of time has made impatience a virtue. There are limitless specific examples of our growing impatience and need for instant gratification, with perhaps the ultimate symbol being the credit card, but in this case the larger dynamics are more telling than the specifics. The best example of our impatience is the way, when looking at how people lived in the past, the modern person is amazed that everyone in the pre-industrial era wasn't bored to death. Forget television – most people could not afford books. So what did they do all day? Well, the fact is that they were not bored, and on balance, we are the ones with the problem. Extending from the matter of impatience, we are incapable of focus, we exhibit short attention spans, and our memory is abysmal. A person could argue that people before simply had less to focus on, less to pay attention to, and less to remember, but that would be precisely the point – we have too much to deal with.

As noted, our fractional perception of time was originally created to facilitate industry, to ensure that workers would do as much as humanly possible. The machine was set to push people to their limits, and we have become so accustomed to it, in fact enraptured with the thrill of our interaction with the machine – through our cars and our computers – that we now accept it without question. So we do have more to pay attention to than people in the past did, but it is too much more. It is more than we were originally designed by nature to deal with. With the distortion of time itself creating stress, the extreme number of things we are expected to pay attention to is even more unnerving. It also prevents us from actually thinking through things, so that we are physically, emotionally, and mentally very active, but the quality of what we think and do is seriously undermined by the quantity.

Except in very specific cases such as the loss of a loved one or another unforeseen disaster, stress can be understood as having more to do than can be dealt with effectively. Ultimately, the manifestation of stress is when one or more of the things a person has to do fails to be accomplished, or it lacks acceptable quality. The first tangible thing that people sacrifice is sleep. Even if a person does not willingly reduce the quantity of sleep he or she gets, the quality of sleep will be reduced due to the stress, and a person's health is subsequently compromised. Typically, the next clear problem occurs in relationships with others, and it is no coincidence that new attitudes toward sexuality and divorce have come at a time when our perception of time demands increasingly instant gratification and a high level of impatience.

The essential point is that we are a world in a hurry, even when we are sleeping. We are in a hurry as a child in school, and even more so as we deal with the hassles of modern life. The fuel of such a society is coffee and lots of sugar, perhaps in the form of a donut, or for kids in the form of sodas. During the average day, a person will break laws – including the speed limit and jaywalking – in order to save a minute of travel time. Those who do not rush are accorded scorn, and on the road are the source of agitation and maneuvering.

But even in times of rest and supposed relaxation, our haste is apparent. Consider television and the way it plays into short attention spans. Advertisements are thirty seconds apiece, exactly. A person is bombarded with images because it would take too long to describe things in words. Complex news stories and political positions have to be condensed into "soundbites" lest the viewer's attention wavers and changes the channel. While it seems natural and beneficial to take in such vast amounts of information quickly, and that the visual

Time and the Human Condition

culture is an improvement over previous methods of communicating information, it is difficult for the human mind to actually process information that quickly – to understand it and learn from it. You experience the information, but have to accept it at face value without reflection, because you will otherwise miss other information. Again, the quantity is high, but the quality is not.

Consider the actual acting – the purely human element – in action movies. Action movies use quick sequences of visual effects that are, in their own way, artistic, but the actors can be positively robotic in their ability to communicate. Contrast recent movies to those made fifty years ago, when people were not as fully conditioned to watch time as we are now, and you will see that the camera stays on the faces of actors longer in older movies. The camera wants to capture the subtle emotion on the face, the depth of acting, and is not concerned about attention spans being too short to stand fixation on a face for more than ten seconds. In movies of the past decade, or perhaps longer, it is standard cinematic practice to move from image to image quickly, and even in a drama a ten second hold would be intolerable. Clearly, our new sense of time has affected our leisure in such a way that we are not allowed to process anything, including earnest human emotion. Emotions in movies today have to be extreme to be recognized, as if we had returned to the day of the silent movies when the art of movie making was just starting to define itself. If the trend continues, everything in movies will become sterile, repetitive, and mechanical. The question is, will anybody notice? A better question, have we already gotten to that point, and simply haven't figured it out?

So, not only do we have to be aware of the nature of time, but we also have to be attentive about what we do with it. In order to learn from our experiences and be able to examine carefully the world around us, and the universe beyond, we need to temporarily live in natural time rather than watch time, lest we accumulate quantity without quality. While it is impossible for a person living in an industrialized society to completely go back to natural time, it is possible to make a limited return to analyze situations with greater attentiveness. A person might be capable of this without any guidance, but more likely either a physical removal out to the countryside or a mental removal from society facilitated by a teacher – of any kind, spiritual or temporal.

Even normal teachers have the ability to present new perspectives to students and improve their quality of thought, if the teacher has that purpose in mind from the start. College, after all, is a state of physical and mental removal from the rest of society that is deliberately built in that manner to facilitate improved modes of thought in a low-stress environment. Few college students actually take advantage of the situation they are presented with, and most that do become professors. Observers from the outside may complain of an academic ivory tower, but the disconnect is the fault of those who perpetuate a system where most people are too stressed to think, not those few who manage to put some quality into their thought.

Before we can widen out perspectives and get a better sense of time, we have to find time in which to contemplate existence. Some people set aside a time to meditate, or plan a retreat for a weekend, and that will do some good, but it is easy to see that in their attempt to escape stress, they continue to be tied to watch time. It is absurd to schedule activities in a vacation, much less a retreat, because that actually perpetuates the underlying structure, the mechanical attitude, which is causing stress. Similarly, anyone that plans to meditate for fifteen minutes, or actually sets a clock nearby to ensure the meditation does not occupy too much of their time, clearly needs to consider what they are trying to rise above, and what they are trying to achieve.

Time and the Human Condition

On the Nature of Philosophy

After the detailed discussion of the nature of perspectives and the four apparent levels of perspective, it should be obvious by the context of this work itself that one area at least does not fit neatly into one level of perspective or another – philosophy. So what is philosophy? Is it something above the four levels, such that it can criticize and examine all of them? Definitely not, since to even claim to be above perspective in this universe, philosophy must claim a source of knowledge outside of this universe, and only spirituality makes that claim, and does so on the basis of faith. Philosophy operates in all levels of perspective, but does so in very particular ways that make it sometimes complementary, and often critical, to personal experience, the dominant culture, the existing understanding of history, and spirituality. Seeing how philosophy interacts with each of these will lend greater clarity to its nature.

Conveniently, philosophers have typically been very specific about what level of understanding they were referring to, so it is actually very straightforward to sort out the operant interactions. Epistemology, for instance, is the philosophy of how knowledge itself is brought about. For instance, Locke's work on human understanding, describing sensation and reflection, is epistemology. While it may be applicable in a broad sense to the entire human race, epistemology is ultimately a matter for the individual. It deals with how an individual comes to know things, and how valid that knowledge might be. It is clearly a matter of personal experience, and a critique of that experience, though the choices allowed to the individual will be influenced by culture, history, and the individual's beliefs about the eternal. Most areas of logic are examinations of the personal level of knowledge in the same manner. This straightforwardness is characteristic of all philosophy because of the emphasis on precise definition.

Aesthetics is concerned with wider dynamics. When the philosopher examines what is considered beautiful, he or she is not typically interested in what is considered beautiful by a single person. Rather, at issue is what makes something beautiful to people in general. The question is what qualities will many people acknowledge as being pleasing to the senses. In almost all cases, this should be considered a matter of culture. The bulk of aesthetics is active at a cultural level, with deep divides between cultures. There are, however, arguments that extend to the historical level, pointing to a few characteristics that can touch people of widely differing cultures, and those are perhaps the most interesting elements of aesthetics. Whatever might be said, though, there are no eternally applicable aesthetics for obvious reasons – we would require contact with an alien species with to establish such truly eternal fundamentals of beauty, if there are any.

To show how a single school of philosophy, rather than an entire area of philosophy, interacts with perspective, we can make use of the example of utilitarianism. Utilitarian arguments, stating that actions should be judged by their utility in bringing about the greatest happiness of the greatest number, have to be either cultural or historical in perspective. Utilitarianism cannot be operant at the individual level, because that would ignore the happiness of the greatest number. So, it requires at least a cultural perspective to take into account an adequate number of individuals to draw conclusions about actions. It also cannot operate at the eternal level for the simple reason that the utility of certain actions can change dramatically when large stretches of time are considered. It would be impossible to analyze the utility of actions beyond historical time, because without sentient humans who can act and based on whom we can judge the utility of the act, such arguments would be groundless.

Moving on, the historical level of philosophy is dominated by political philosophy. Most philosophers, and in particular Plato, Aristotle, Hobbes, and Locke, set forth political principles based on their conclusions in other areas of philosophy. For instance, Locke developed conclusions on human understanding, and from those conclusions derived his political philosophy Politics can be clearly seen as functioning on the historical level of perspective. In fact, history is completely dominated by political issues and movements, and only recently has there been added attention to economics and social dynamics. Politics cannot be eternal for the simple reason that no state in history has shown the ability to last for even a decent fraction of human history, much less given any sign of being eternal. Political systems must also transcend culture. Their relative longevity gives them legitimacy and resistance to the whims of mainstream culture. In both the Roman and modern eras of multiculturalism, the political realm has been required to keep cultures from conflict, and needs to work at a broader level of perspective, or it will be the tool of one culture or another.

But most of philosophy tries to make general arguments that are meant to be solid in all cases, transcending even the presence of the human species. Metaphysics is the most immediate example of philosophy at the level of eternal perspective, but so is Ethics. While at face value Ethics might seem to require the presence of human beings, the fact is that it is composed of abstract ideas that, to be correct, must have value even without the existence of beings capable of being ethical. After all, there might never have been a purely ethical human being (a subject of some debate), so without a level of abstraction beyond the actual history of humanity, there would be only fragmentary examples of ethical life. We would have examples of individual actions, but such detached actions would not suggest a uniform mode of appropriate action that can infuse an entire life. Ethics must be eternal, because there is little evidence of it in history, culture, or personal experience.

Most philosophical schools do the bulk of their work at the eternal level of perspective. Whether it is through Determinism, Epicureanism, Fatalism, Idealism, Materialism, Naturalism, or so many other collections of thought, philosophy makes certain claims about the eternal nature of the universe. The strongest school of eternal inquiry is that of the inductive natural philosophers – science. Following the pattern of Newton, natural philosophers derived conclusions about the eternal universe, coming up with understandings like gravity that are far beyond the limitations of history. Science can confine itself to very specific phenomenon that occur at the level of individual experience, but it is almost never concerned with ideas on the cultural or historical scale, and most often draws conclusions that give perspective on the eternal. Since the start of the twentieth century, science has not been commonly associated with philosophy, but it can still be shown to have a similar relationship to perspective. Apart from public perception, the major difference between philosophy and science is that science has decided on a definite system of experimentation through which the nature of the universe might be known, while philosophy has multiple models that may never be synthesized into a single view.

The position of philosophy is always as something on the outside. Even though the thinking of philosophers is very much affected by context, it is expected of philosophers that they try their best to rise above that context to gain perspective and move the human race along on the quest for truth. This position is perfectly safe as long as philosophy agrees with the dominant model at each level of perspective. Philosophy and science can agree with the mainstream spirituality – as shown by Descartes, Locke, and Newton in the case of Christianity. Or, they can be in opposition to the spiritual understanding of the time – Galileo, Spinoza, and Voltaire come to mind.

When philosophy disagrees with widely held ideas at any level of perspective, it can generate great discontent and opposition. Sometimes, this leads to persecution. But this is true when any competing models of truth face each other – there will be conflict. However, because philosophy is characterized by its outsider nature, it tends to lead more to a war of words than a real war. There will be resentment, and accusations that the philosophy is out of touch with reality, but since the end of the medieval age, philosophers have basically been left to their own devices. The struggles over science are a more recent example, with some cultures within the United States seeing science as at odds with their understanding of reality, while other parts of American society have no idea what the fuss is about. Whatever the gap in understanding, it will not cause the kind of wars other ideologies (in some cases, philosophies taken to irrational extremes) might generate.

If philosophy and science can operate at more than one level of perspective, why doesn't spirituality? This can best be explained in terms of purpose. It is spirituality's express purpose to focus on the questions of eternity, the afterlife, and the divine realms, and to only discuss matters of this world when they relate to issues of the divine plane. Philosophy and science, on the other hand, are on a quest for knowledge. That is the literal meaning of philosophy – love of knowledge. It is not that those involved in spirituality are incapable of considering all levels of perspective, but rather that their efforts have been directed in a more focused direction. Spirituality's focus often renders it susceptible to considerations of the lower perspectives – including involvement in cultural struggles and political wars – but those are distractions from the stated purpose. Those distractions often confuse followers, not to mention later generations looking on critically, in a completely needless way. Even worse, such deviations from the purpose of spirituality can also lead to hypocrisies and the contradiction of doctrine, breaking down the foundations of belief.

Philosophy has other troubles. Its virtue is in its lack of focus, and its ability to synthesize knowledge derived from many areas, but over time as knowledge accumulates, that synthesis grows more and more difficult. Instead of synthesis, specialization develops. People are familiar with this trend in science, where the fast growth of knowledge has led to specialization of research to a degree that even people well acquainted with biology, physics, chemistry, or any other area might have difficulty understanding the implications of a particular paper or experiment in that same area. It may be impossible for a single person to understand developments in all the frontiers of science. Yet, science is grounded in concrete phenomena. The rest of philosophy was abstract to begin with, and has only become more difficult for the average person to get a grasp of. Unlike the direct understanding and prescriptions provided by spirituality, philosophy can become too wide-ranging to practically apply in an internally consistent manner. In other words, far from simply being accused of irrelevance by those that disagree with its methods, philosophy really can become irrelevant if it does not somehow bring together its conclusions in each of the levels of perspective and apply the newly synthesized knowledge. As the example of the foundation of the United States based on philosophical principles – such as Natural Rights and the social contract – shows, such an application of knowledge can have powerful and long-lasting significance.

Time and the Human Condition

So, while it might be ideal for spirituality to focus on the eternal, and for philosophers to synthesize all levels of knowledge, each will trend to diverge from the ideal until redirected by some seminal figure. Spirituality will involve itself in mundane matters, and the marketplace will be placed at the steps of the temple, until a prophet redraws the line between the two. Philosophy will become specialized, with philosophers considering only parts of all knowledge that has come before, until an Aristotle or Francis Bacon comes along and organizes it all in their minds, placing their stamp on all areas of knowledge for centuries to come.

Human Understanding

Time and Love

Perhaps the brightest point in the human condition, insofar as it is experienced on Earth, is the capacity for, and sharing of, love. Discussing love in terms of time and perspective might seem to be the height of absurdity, but there are a few points of interest that can be used as a way of understanding the larger dynamics. Needless to say, I will not attempt to wax eloquent about the beauty and importance of love, nor examine what love is, or how it might be obtained. These are questions of individual experience, and judging from the sheer mass of discourse on love – scholarly, artistic, and casual – highly dependent on the quality of that experience. What can be considered, however, is how love works at different levels, and in fact is closely related to matters of identity and conflicts concerning identity.

    Love, as it will be understood in the discussion that follows, is essentially voluntary. Five types of love will be discussed – love between two individuals (which will be called basic love), friendship, love of culture, love of country, and love of the eternal. The first two are associated with the individual experience level of perspective, while each of those that follow match up with the cultural, historical, and eternal respectively. Though there may be pressures placed upon a person to engage in certain kinds of relationships with an individual, a culture, a nation, and a spiritual system, there is no way for something external to a person to force a person to love any of these things. Love is entirely an internal matter, and if it is shared, that sharing does not occur in a tangible manner. There is one form of love commonly acknowledged that will not be discussed – love of family. It will not be discussed because its very nature is dependant on culture, its foundation is established by birth and not by choice, and historically it was considered a matter of duty and piety, not of love. The dynamics of the family are also complicated by the basic love held by the two parents, and the way the love of family can collapse if this basic love no longer exists, or never existed. It is conceivable that, for siblings, love of family is actually a form of friendship, though a form that is stronger purely because of the time spent in the friendship and the bonds that have been built in that time. Any deeper analysis of the love of family is difficult for the reasons described above.

    The form of love we immediately consider when the term is brought up is the love between two individuals that is of such a quality that they would choose to live together for the rest of their lives. The strength of this fundamental form of love is partly in its exclusivity – each individual can only share this kind of love with one other individual at a given time. If a person has a relationship with two others, then that person's love is necessarily divided, if only because the love for one is tainted by the guilt felt for infidelity toward the other. In the ideal, this form of love will bring together two individuals so that they can work towards a common purpose, and that purpose is traditionally to show care for the next generation, but it is ultimately so that neither of the individual is alone and adrift in the world. Human beings are social creatures. We show it in our capacity for love and our need for love. It is our social nature, and not the practical need to care for the next generation, that predetermines that individuals will go through life in pairs. The need to care for the next generation alone is not adequate explanation for love at this level, as shown by the great number of people who marry, have children, and divorce. A marriage can fail despite the presence of children if the social imperative of our nature is not fulfilled by the relationship – if love is not present. Of course, the ideal purpose would combine the social, which is essentially the selfish purpose of love, and the practical, which is the tangible product of a fruitful relationship – though not directly related to the love itself.

That being said, it should be clear that this form of love is limited by the lifespan of each individual. Whatever romantics might claim, influenced perhaps by the power of love, even the vows of marriage note that the union ends with death. Love at this level is a matter of individual experience, and subsequently demands that level of perspective to function. Of course, this means that everyone that exists in the universe, and can build individual experience, has the capacity to create a loving relationship with another. Can love be limited by the lack of perspective, then? Definitely. In fact, divorce is often caused by actions that take into consideration extremely narrow senses of time. This is not to say that there are not legitimate grounds for divorce, not to mention that people only get married when they feel the bonds of love. However, our current high divorce rate is caused by more than abuse or impulsive marriage. That divorce rate began rising before the women's rights movement of the sixties and seventies, so that spurious argument can be rejected offhand. The increase in the divorce rate did, on the other hand, start at about the same time as the mechanization of time began – at the end of the nineteenth century. The connection between the perception of time and the nature of love is essential to understanding modern dynamics around love. If a person is unable to think beyond, say, a few weeks' time, there is a great deal of strife that may occur in a relationship that is expected to last a lifetime. What might actually be minor issues and arguments when looking at an entire life can seem to be huge and insurmountable obstacles when only a few weeks are considered at a time.

Time and the Human Condition

Recall the discussion about time and stress. If the mechanization of time can produce stress in an individual because it forces the individual into an unnatural understanding of time, then what effect does the modern sense of time have on a natural function like love? To put it simply, the segmentation of time, which puts stress on the individual, puts similar stress on love. This does not include the impact that the individual's own stress might have on the relationship, but instead takes the relationship between two individuals as an independent dynamic. The nature of that dynamic itself changes as the perception of time at the two ends of the dynamic – the two individuals – changes. Again, this is most clearly manifested in the way minor issues, for instance money matters, can become reasons for divorce. The unnatural sense of time distorts the situation. Surely, the ties that bind individuals together should be able to overcome such transitory problems as matters of money, but not if the individuals engaged in love are incapable of perceiving, in the moment of strife, those lifelong bonds. And certainly, not when the culture surrounding the two individuals puts more emphasis on money than on love, and downplays the power of love while boasting of the power of money.

We will move onto the cultural level in a moment, but there is an important intermediary level in the spectrum of love that also operates at the level of individual experience – friendship. There is no question in the general discourse that friendship includes a far less intense version of what would otherwise be considered love. In fact, when a person splits his or her primary capacity for loving relationship, as described above, between two or more people, it might be argued that neither relationship goes beyond the level of friendship in all but the physical sense. There are also limits to how thinly friendship can be spread – a person might have a dozen or so real friends at most, but beyond that the associations are noticeably too shallow to be called friendship. Of all the levels of love, friendship is the least intense, and therefore the least affected by changes in perceptions of time. It is the least intense because, though it operates at the level of individual experience, it is still essentially a love between two individuals, and does not have the collective strength of more dissipated levels of love, but also is not exclusive and undivided like the basic primary love between two individuals. In fact, basic love can distract a person from friendships without any adverse consequences. Friendships can break down without great strife, and they can form without any ritual.

The cultural level of love is the least considered, because only recently have cultures become geographically intermingled. Through most of history, with the possible exception of Rome, cultures were geographically confined. There was also a certain understanding that each person would consider his own culture natural, and so there would be no sense to criticize the cultures of others. When ideas were spread, it was primarily by merchants and travelers, so that there was time for cultures to assimilate new ideas based on utility and interest without unbalancing themselves and creating strife. Today, however, the love of one's culture must be examined because near-instantaneous communication has brought ideas head-to-head without allowing time for consideration of ideas, thereby spurring on greater strife. Since travel became quick and easy in the late nineteenth century, and the Europeans brought themselves into close contact with cultures around the world, there has been an era of cultural intolerance that would have shocked the ancients. So, let us take a look at this love of culture and how the so-called culture wars operate.

People have no trouble understanding love of music or art, and often those things can be more closely related to an individual than his or her friends are. While the arts are definitely factors of culture, they are also transcendent and in touch with the spiritual, so that they cannot be put forward as examples of cultural love. That is not a problem since practically any time a person is part of a group and does not personally know all the members, that person is engaged in cultural activity because culture is, by definition, what mediates between the individuals in the group. Any attachment a person has to a particular group identity can be called cultural love. When people talk about 'corporate culture,' this can be taken quite literally, though love of corporate cultures has been declining sharply since the start of the Great Depression. It is doubtful that all but the founding members of a company now feel any strong attachment to it, at least not compared to that felt by workers before the Great Depression, but there was a time when corporate culture was a strong influence in a person's cultural identity. Group identity is far from the sole form of cultural love, but it is the most blatant. At the subtle level, the way a person uses language is itself a matter of cultural identity, and certain accents or mannerisms can be so tightly tied to identity that a person would not be the same without them.

So, what are the culture wars? To put it simply, it is when the norms one large cultural group establishes for itself disagrees with the norms of another group in the same geographical area, and one or both of the groups appeal to the higher level of perspective, the political realm, to push the society as a whole toward their point of view. This is a natural process, and it is the burden of politics to ensure that it is not swayed to benefit one view or the other, or even intervene to make a determination that would affect the entire society, unless it is absolutely necessary. In general, it is only necessary when the competing views might resort to violence. After all, whatever the government's decision might be, it will probably satisfy only a minority of those who care, so reluctance to intervene is justified.

Lest we lapse into more obvious and contemporary examples, as have been discussed in relation to the culture wars in other sections, consider the struggle between management and labor, particularly at the end of the nineteenth century and the start of the twentieth. In the old labor struggles, corporate managers represented a culture of laissez-faire capitalism, and adhered to the principle that their efforts to turn a profit were actually to the benefit of society. Corporate culture, from the point of view of management, was a hierarchical one in which those at the top necessarily knew what was best for everyone in the company, and that economical wisdom was what mediated relationships between the individuals in the company. After all, if they did not have that wisdom, they would not have reached the top in the first place. Labor, on the other hand, had a range of different ideas about how the culture of the working world should be, from simply securing the right to complain, to unionizing, to socialism. This spread of ideas, often associated with the different ethnic background and therefore the different values of the workers, is the reason why labor has never been strong in the United States, compared to the labor parties and firm unions in other nations. Management had, ultimately, a single set of cultural ideas, while labor was divided by many conceptions, so that there was a great deal of internal strife in and among the unions.

So, the struggle between management and labor can be understood as a type of culture war. Here are two groups with different conceptions about the way things ought to be. It should be made clear that management did not simply invent an artificial understanding to cloak what they actually understood to be devious and unsupportable – they believed in their views as much as labor did. The labor wars were vital to the livelihood of at least one of the two groups, and so quickly grew in intensity from a war of words to real violence. Between sabotage and assassinations on the one hand and police brutality and rigged prosecution on the other, it was clear that the political realm would have to step in. When it did, though, it initially put down the unions and favored management outright. Needless to say, this did not end up producing a stabilizing result. Festering safely below the radar during the twenties, the labor movements reemerged during the Great Depression. The local and state governments were still on the side of management, but the federal government, under President Franklin Roosevelt, finally gave unions some rights. While there was, and still is, strife between labor and management, nothing after the legalization of unions matched the wars that occurred before it.

To understand all of this in terms of cultural love, it is necessary to focus in on the labor unions. There was, within these organizations, a strong sense of identification and a push for solidarity. In some extreme unions, like the International Workers of the World, getting married was actually shunned, since it would make a worker more dependant on steady pay and therefore more susceptible to management. When in the midst of struggles, cultural groups can demand great sacrifices of their members, and increase the degree the individual looks for friends within rather than outside the group. There are two main ways cultural groups split – either the group is deemed by some ineffective in its purpose, or it is too extreme in its demands on its members. The charge of ineffectiveness often hinges on attempts to change the identity of the group. The dynamics of cultural love are complicated, but this level of love can have profound influence on the individual. Even the weakest cultural connections and identifications can outright determine the kind of friends a person might have, and limit a person's perceived prospects for marriage.

Human Understanding

In the contemporary world, the culture wars revolve around such issues as abortion, school prayers, and gay marriage. On what has been defined as the conservative side (on the issue of school prayers, this side is technically liberal since it emphasizes the personal freedom to pray), the issues are typically framed in religious terms, and more or less unified as a single cultural vision. It is important to note, though, that this is an example of spirituality getting caught up in a cultural conflict, and not spirituality itself. The liberal side is, on the other hand, more diffuse on each of these issues. And, though it may seem a coarse way to discuss it, each side adheres to its position with a fervency that can only be a form of love, attachment, and identification. As is characteristic of the culture wars, both sides are appealing to the political level. That, in fact, is what shows this to be a cultural issue – if it was anything else, the two sides would not look to the historical level of perspective to resolve the issue. While one side might attempt to justify its position spiritually, true spiritual or eternal matters can only be resolved outside of this universe – there is no higher understanding or perspective within this universe to appeal to.

When thinking about the culture wars, it is vital to remember that they are recent developments. Before the modern age of travel and communication, there was time to deal with new ideas, but now there is no such time. At the cultural level, the shortening of travel and communication times is equivalent to the fragmented and mechanical sense of time examined in terms of stress and the basic loving relationship. It produces the same increased stress, and this stress takes the form of two lovers fighting over the hearts and minds of society. The speed of communication hinders understanding, so that there is a greater quantity of communication, but decreased quality. Simple misunderstanding, though, cannot be blamed for all cultural conflicts. Rather, the emotion associated with lack of understanding – fear – is to blame.

The political realm, to which opposing cultures and individuals attempt to appeal, is only a part of the historical perspective. However, it is the only part that establishes identity, and subsequently attracts another kind of love. In this case, the love is instantly identifiable – love of country, national pride, and patriotism. It is a very diffuse form of love, but one made potent by the sheer numbers involved. In political systems with no attempt at political representation or involvement, the relationship between the individual and the country is weak. Before the seventeenth century, society was more locally focused, so that people were not very attached to the historical in comparison to the individual level, culture, and spirituality. When the political realm is more open to and involved with the population, people become more attached to their country, and patriotism is fostered. It is no coincidence that nationalism was first developed in the French Revolution, when literally everyone in France was eventually mobilized and involved in the tumult of the country, and that Napoleon would eventually wield that nationalism to create his army, the largest seen up to that point in Europe.

Since then, leaders have become more attentive to the population, feeling the need to draw people into politics. Dictators resort to propaganda in the modern world for the same reason, though primarily to build large armies (in general, armies of a number greater than one percent of the nation's population) and maintain morale within them in imitation of Napoleon's achievement. It is the notion of representation and involvement within the government that is important to build patriotism, not actual representation. So long as people feel that they have a stake in the political realm, they will have a strong national identity even without actually voting for leaders or for legislation. In a true representative system, though, love of country is more than a byproduct, but rather essential for the proper running of the system. Being able to determine the course of their nation, people have to consider the overall welfare of the nation above all else. This, of course, is never the case, and voters are plagued with their individual needs, cultural norms, and spiritual imperatives. However, if they were only concerned with those three levels, the system would break down. People would not respect the decision of the political realm in relation to their other concerns, and would rebel against it. There would be constant civil war. Love of country ensures that, even if the vote goes against their own personal needs, people will not rebel against the government and will abide by the decision of the population as a whole.

The problems of patriotism are the same as those in the lower levels of perception. The fragmentation of time and the high speed of communication ensure that people do not have time to digest the massive matters of history – and given the breadth and depth of historical affairs, it would be difficult for people to get a grasp of affairs in the first place. It is painfully easy for people to become fearful, and to react out of fear in political matters. Fear is more potent at this level, though, because leaders can wield it to their advantage, while cultural dynamics are far more difficult to steer. Early conflict between countries was a matter of resources, and in that respect completely natural in fulfilling the purpose of society – to seek the greatest welfare for the individuals within it. Since the development of nationalism, however, ideology has come into play as the major point of conflict. Some political scientists like to project this back on the past, or apply the resource argument on the present, but while such interpretation may be true in very specific situations, or in the minds of certain individuals, it is generally incorrect.

And why has ideology become a flashpoint? Of course, because the communication of ideas has become so fast that there is no chance for gradual adaptation to new modes of thought, and reactions based on emotion, and particularly fear, dominate. This, and the increased speed of transportation, is why wars since the United States Civil War, which was deeply ideologically driven, have been unusually frequent compared to the rest of history. The bloodiness of wars might be a factor of new technology, but it is also a matter of the number of people fighting and the willingness to attack civilian targets. As previously noted, the number of people fighting has increased by means of nationalism and patriotism in the Napoleonic model. The willingness to attack civilian targets is precisely due to the shift from wars for resource to wars of ideology. If the enemy is an ideological threat to you, that threat does not emanate only from the armies of the enemy, but from the very minds of every person on the enemy side. On the other hand, resources can be obtained without killing the civilian population, which poses no threat to a claim, and even in the worst situation they can simply be forced to leave their homes. In ancient times, of course, the civilians were often enslaved, so we should not assign moral superiority to one form of war too quickly. However, it is possible to determine in modern times whether a war is for resources or for ideology simply by noting if either side deliberately attacks civilians. After determining the nature of the war as ideological, though, a person has to be careful to decide what ideology is being contested, especially since leaders of each side will spread disinformation about the issue.

The love and conflict operant at the historical level is well known and the subject of intense study. At the eternal level, it can get impossibly complicated. A person might express love for God, but this can only be considered love at the eternal level if God is considered the universe itself. If God is outside of the universe, or its creator, then love for God is only possible outside of the universe. So what people in spirituality actually love is the concept of God, the idea of God, which exists at the eternal level of perception within the universe. As if this was not complicated enough, some religions – Catholicism included – emphasize the need for an individual relationship with the divine. The need for a relationship with God at the basic level is the reason why the Catholic clergy is forbidden from marrying and must remain celibate – lest they divide their love at the basic level and deny God the full measure of it. It is clear, however, that love at the eternal level is usually only possible through spirituality of some sort. Only the rare individual will feel anything comparable to love while examining the eternal through science, and though philosophy technically means love of knowledge, true philosophers in this sense are also hard to find.

Spiritual love is difficult to discuss because it is often complicated by interactions with the other levels. It is easy to see that religion can transcend national boundaries, and that there are religious wars, but true religious wars are actually very rare. Wars that are supposedly for spiritual reasons are more often actually for resources or political ideology. The Christian Crusades during the Middle Ages were true religious wars – the ultimate religious authority of Christianity at the time – the Pope – called for them, not a mere political leader or anyone unfit to speak for the entire religion, and they were launched at great cost and for no political gain purely on a spiritual belief about the Holy Land. In contrast, the Thirty Years War from 1618 to 1648 in Europe, which pitted Protestants against Catholics, was not a religious war. Its beginnings were purely political – a matter of succession – and no recognized spiritual leader engaged the fight solely on the basis of religion. The only religious leader directly involved – Cardinal Richelieu – actually played both sides against each other to gain resources, including political influence. The Thirty Years War was nevertheless important for the status of

Protestantism, so it had a religious impact without being a religious war. In general, any war in which one side or another is seeking gains outside of spiritual purpose should not be considered a religious war, though it can still be a war of ideology.

Some readers might have noticed that, since war is technically at the historical level of understanding, spiritual systems are actually narrowing their perspective when they oppose each other violently. For the eternal perspective, the ideal mode of opposition is that taken in philosophy or science – calm scholarly discourse. The use of warfare often has the result of perverting spiritual beliefs, leading to contradictions and hypocrisies built in the heat of conflict. The economics of war can also make a spiritual system beholden to the wealthy who fund the war, so that special spiritual conditions may pertain to those with enough money to pay for them. Any spiritual system takes an immense and often irreversible risk by resorting to war.

Are conflicts of spiritual love influenced by the modern sense of time? The rapid exchange of ideas can certainly have an impact on spiritual understanding, but the impact is so confused with culture and political ideology that sorting modern trends can become immensely difficult. More often than not, spirituality is used to justify a cultural or political position. The fragmentation of time has ensured that spiritual leaders are less able to resist becoming involved in cultural and historical matters. Those who advise and inform the faithful are as affected by the fragmentation as anyone else in society, and it ensures that they are driven more by emotion than by careful thought when considering new ideas. Interestingly, the effect of the modern sense of time on spiritual thought is far less serious than the effect of conflict. Even the incidental effects of religious conflict can be tremendously dangerous and regrettable. For example, the tensions of the

Reformation, when Catholics and Protestant fought openly, led to a dramatic increase in witch trials and the deaths of over ten thousand individuals on hearsay evidence. The modern sense of time alone has not led to anything in spirituality nearly so destructive.

Love operates at each level of perspective, and in every case it is subjected to the way time is perceived. While at first people think only of the basic relationship when love is mentioned, the full scope of love is clear when love of country and love of the divine are mentioned. The nature of love itself can be difficult to penetrate – it is intangible, and is distinct from the relationships and physical acts that are a product of it – so it becomes necessary to explain it by example. Nevertheless, even more unanswerable questions arise when any explanation is attempted. In relation to time, a person might wonder whether love has any direct relation to time, since the perception of time has such an influence on the nature of love, and the different ways love can operate. Dealing with the love of God, a person might wonder about its timelessness and to what degree it might be manifest in the universe. The entire issue of being unable to love God, and only being able to love the idea of God, is certain to be disputed for the problems it causes. Of all topics relating to the human condition, love is the most vexing in this way, though perhaps its mystery is what invites romantic notions and gives it power.

Conclusion
Means Without Ends

To decide on an end toward which we can move, we have to limit our perspective and narrow the sense of time we take into consideration. We cannot conclude an ultimate end for our own lives, and subsequently work toward that goal, because we lack knowledge about the purpose of our creation and other key pieces of information. We can only assume goals like reaching heaven or ending the cycle of reincarnation on the basis of faith, since we cannot know that either is the definitive end we should aim for. And, of course, we cannot base a conclusion about the human condition on faith, since there are many different things people around the world have faith in. Only knowledge of the universe's purpose would eliminate such disagreement. If we had such information, then we could confidently progress to the logical end for which we were created. Without that knowledge, our lives will inevitably be a search. We can only act based on limited understanding, and therefore must either confine ourselves to short-term ends or abandon the idea that the means we employ need to work to a known goal.

If we want to move beyond our existing understanding and the current limitations on our perspective, we have to understand that the process cannot have a predetermined end. Firm ends can only be envisioned based on existing knowledge. If we want true progress, we will only have a vague view of what the end might look like. In other words, every time a person wants to increase his or her understanding, he or she is

Conclusion

taking a risk. If it is an honest attempt at personal progress, there is always the risk that the person's existing understanding of some matter might be challenged. Picking up the pieces of old ideas in the face of new information is always unpleasant, and is often misconstrued as a step back. People tend to avoid this risk whenever possible.

The vagueness of ends is particularly noticeable in true revolutions. A revolutionary might seek a democratic government, but would not be able to define the particulars. It is common in the study of revolutions to discuss a structure – anti-structure – structure pattern, and it is in the anti-structure period that no clear end is in sight, and literally anything can happen. In the case of the American Revolution, the vagueness over ends left the nation under the excessively weak Articles of Confederation. So, from 1776 to 1787, the United States was very much in the anti-structure phase of the revolution. It was only after much debate at the Constitutional Convention in 1787, during which the vagueness of the new system was eliminated and a more solid view of the revolution's end was formed, that the Constitution was written. During the revolution itself, no one could have said what the product of the war would look like.

It is also absurd to talk about ends justifying means in all but the most specific scopes and confined perspectives. In a period of intense change, the means must justify themselves. By the very nature of the modern day, as described in "Time and Stress", we are faced with constant intense change in comparison with what was faced two hundred years ago. We can rarely see the end of anything, even if it lies only a week or a month away, so we have to be careful to choose an unimpeachable set of means – which, as will soon be clear, is composed of means that do no appreciable harm to others. Historically, it is a strong criticism of revolutions that they often fail to determine the means by which they will proceed

Time and the Human Condition

in a firm way. The French Revolution is the most significant example of a set of revolutionaries failing to define themselves, and subsequently falling to a new group with a clear agenda but brutal means.

But is it possible for means to justify themselves? Naturally, it can. In fact, the idea that ends justify the means is a Machiavellian innovation adopted by modern politics. Ideally, the means should always justify themselves. When Machiavelli, at the start of the sixteenth century, wrote his view of politics, he was describing what he saw as the actual situation. He noticed that, both in history and in Italy at the time, successful leaders rarely acted according to the ideal, and more often followed what we today call realist politics – "realpolitik". In trying to improve our situation and understanding, though, we are necessarily interested in the elusive ideal. Basing our actions on what has worked so far can only perpetuate the current situation, which is, by all accounts, improvable.

For a quick example of how means can justify themselves, consider nonviolent protest. No matter what the ends are, nonviolent protest is beyond reproach. Whether it is necessary is another question, but there should be no need to defend nonviolence as a means. Contrast it with war. War must always be justified before it is embarked upon not only by its ends, but also by an inciting incident. In fact, many would argue that no war is justifiable, but no one will reasonably suggest that all war is justified without exception.

How can nonviolence be ethically correct by definition if there is no universally agreed upon set of ethics? It is because, by definition, nonviolence does no harm. That is the overriding key, enshrined in both the basic purpose described earlier in this book and the social contract as established by the political philosophers of the seventeenth century – Any use of freedom that does not violate another person's security has passed ethical tests. Nonviolence may not be necessary, and it may not agree with the dominant culture or historical convenience, but it is justified for any end. Perhaps it will be clearer if we define "justified" in terms of justice. Remember that justice, as examined in "On Law, Justice, and Order", is primarily mediating between two ends of a continuum – freedom to (freedom) and freedom from (security). The role of a court is to decide what is just. If one party claims that there is an imbalance between the two poles in a certain situation – that an event is unjust – then the other party must justify the event either by denying his involvement, by showing how it might not be defined as unjust, or by showing that there were special circumstances that would justify his actions. In a murder case, one person took the freedom to kill another, denying the other's security in the penultimate manner. There is no way to redefine murder as just. There may, however, be special circumstances that can justify it – self-defense, for instance. Most often, though, defendants in a murder case will argue that they were not at fault, and avoid the need to justify an act like murder. The less serious the crime, the more room there is for justification.

Bringing this back to nonviolence, it is easy to see why the means of nonviolence, if strictly adhered to, cannot be considered unjust in any case. Some might note that nonviolent movements have always had clear ends in mind, often very specifically, and this is quite true. The reason nonviolence makes for an excellent example and model, though, is that despite having an end in mind, the movements did not take a "by all means necessary" stand. Even though their ends were great goods worthy of immense sacrifice, protesters did not place the burden of that sacrifice on their oppressors. Now, given the standard philosophical position in which no answer can be known and all ends are utopias – visions without any basis in reality – we should be even more careful at selecting means as the protesters for freedom and civil rights were. We can build a set of tools, suggested throughout the previous sections, which will help us make progress to the unknown ends.

The first means introduced in this book was science. Science is a method of inquiry that is limited in its application, but still has wide frontiers to explore. The chapters on physics should have made the philosophical implications of science clear. As for how effective science is at answering questions, increasing our knowledge and perspective, and improving the quality of life (helping us to satisfy our basic needs), we can say that it had done so to widely acclaimed success. Science can be wrong, but at least it doesn't take hundreds of years to admit it. And, since ethical standards were imposed on researchers, it is almost always a self-justified means. The only possible exception is the use of animals in research, in which case scientists actually have to justify the means by pointing to beneficial ends. In physics, geology, and most other areas of science, there is no such research that complicates the self-justification of the method.

Science is part of our overall ability to contemplate eternity. That ability gives rise to a number of different means by which our understanding can grow, including philosophy and spirituality. Whether the different ways that ability manifests itself are self-justified depends on their individual nature. For instance, there were once many spiritual systems that employed human sacrifice to appease the gods. Such systems are obviously not self-justifying. Notice that this does not mean that their means are not justified – for adherents to such a system, the ends of appeasing the gods clearly justify the sacrifice of a single person. Today, we might dispute this justification on a number of grounds, but which view is correct cannot be determined. So, some manifestations of the ability to contemplate eternity will be certain to move us forward and improve our understanding if we employ them, and others

Conclusion

may or may not. Ideally, of course, all spiritual and philosophical systems would be self-justifying – in that they should not advocate harm to others – but this is not the case in practice. In most cases, it is culture and the power relations associated with culture that complicate spiritual and philosophical systems, and reorient them so that they seek justification of means in presumed ends.

After taking a look at possible afterlives and their complications – particularly the problems involving the interaction between spirituality and culture – the qualities that defined a legitimate community were examined. These qualities, when combined, can be thought of as a means that I will call the democratic means. The democratic means therefore is the combined use of freedom of belief, freedom of expression, equality before the law, time to pursue individual happiness, and sustainability. It is called the democratic means because it relies on representative government, and because it is based on a specific interpretation of the social contract.

According to Thomas Hobbes, governments are built through a common agreement called the social contract, with the sole purpose of ensuring the mutual safety of the individuals in the community. Hobbes used this version of the social contract to justify the British monarchy, but it can actually justify practically any kind of government. There has to be a specific reasoning behind representative government that goes beyond Hobbes' formulation, and makes the social contract more specific so that it excludes governments that use the excuse of security to take unjust advantage of the population – the dictatorships in the mid-twentieth century, for instance. The reasoning is actually fairly clear if we take into account both freedom and security. Hobbes only takes security into account, making his theories unbalanced. Governments should actually try to balance the freedom of individuals and their security, rather than simply emphasize security. Can a monarchy or dictatorship attain such a balance? Not easily, since the temptation of power, particularly when only one person is expected to wield it and solve the problems of the nation, is so great. The purpose of representative government is to spread out both the power and the responsibility, so that it will be easier to attain the balance. The idea that a balance between freedom and security must be sought – instead of favoring one or the other – can be called the democratic principle, which modifies the social contract theory of Hobbes. Even representative governments will gradually try to concentrate power in the center in the name of security, though. Representation and the vote can only diffuse and forestall this trend, not completely eliminate it. The democratic means, then, is the tool that the individuals of the community can use to establish and maintain their freedom and restore balance.

Can the democratic means be used for anything else except for keeping the balance? In fact, it is of central importance to all endeavors. Freedom of expression, for instance, is essential for all communication between individuals, not simply for keeping the democratic principle intact. Even if the balance between freedom to and freedom from was guaranteed, that would only make the freedom of expression more useful, since people would no longer be afraid of what some forms of expression might lead to. Communication, in general, is essential to the betterment of the human condition and the base quality of life. We will only develop our ideas through detailed discussion and debate. The fact that, in the mainstream media, detailed and meticulous debate is often replaced by soundbites, irrational argument, and meaningless repetition is a prominent and outstanding fault in the way we communicate ideas. That fault far outweighs the dualistic debate about whether the media has a liberal or conservative bias. The freedom of expression, applied to the fullest reasonable extent, can have a transformative effect that the advent of twenty-

Conclusion

four hour news only hints at. All improvements in the modes of communication have drastic implications for the way we live and think, perhaps second only to improvements in transportation since traveling to other lands is far more powerful an experience than simply hearing about them. Once the democratic principle and means are used to establish legitimate communities, then, they will still be useful to us in the next stage of development and improved understanding.

Comprehending the levels of perspective is a valuable tool to sort out conflicts faced in life. Categorizing conflicts, and specific arguments within conflicts, might seem a frivolous endeavor at the start, but to understand the complex dynamics of thought and conflict in the modern world, we need tools that are generally applicable to sort things out. It seems sometimes that the way people currently think through issues is to put opinions into one of two columns – one titled liberal, the other titled conservative – and are expected to accept one or the other of the columns as a block. Certainly political parties often act as if this was the case, and issues are presented in the media accordingly. To make it possible to get a fuller understanding and a greater breadth of perspectives, we need to take time to consider the issue. That time is not always available, so on an individual basis, we need ways of organizing ideas so we can quickly guess how they interrelate, and so we can see what information might be missing from the picture. The discussion of perspective is one such method of quick organization, and another is presented in the second appendix. Throughout this book, the discussion of perspective has been employed, and the way it has been used should serve as an example. Every person has to find tools that they can understand. Sometimes tools can be found explicitly described in books, but more often only a study of culture, history, and philosophy will yield them. In every case, the goal is to develop a tool that can help a person to seek as many points of view on a particular issue as possible without simply getting confused, and without taking too much time trying to things out. It is impossible to see everything, but it is definitely possible to take into account more than two oversimplified points of view.

The use of historical perspective to understand cultural dynamics was first employed in the section on oral and written tradition. The reason for examining the ancient move from oral to written tradition was twofold. First, it is important for people to realize when studying ancient cultures that they might have had a rich oral tradition that we have very little understanding of. It is common for people studying the ancient world to think of communities that used a written tradition as 'civilized' and to think of those maintaining an oral tradition as 'barbarians'. Eliminating this bias is important for the understanding of cultures through history, since otherwise we would complicate our understanding by valuing some cultures over others, and seeing the triumph of some as 'progress' and of others as a fall.

The second, and more immediate, reason to discuss the way tradition is passed down within a culture is the modern shift from written to visual culture. Television is now a major means of conveying information, and it relies more on visual input than words to make its point. As in the ancient shift, written tradition will not be completely abandoned. A shift in the mode of tradition simply implies that people will reach for, and to a great extent trust, one before the other. In context with the discussion of means, it is clear that the way culture is conveyed can have great influence in how we understand things, and improving the quality of cultural transmission will improve our mutual understanding. It is also essential in the modern age of global media that there is proper balance. It is striking in some countries around the world how little time is spent on international news in the media. Twenty-four hour news in the United States spends hours a day analyzing the most inconsequential court cases, and ignores news that is perceived to be less entertaining. Entertainment can be one consideration, but cannot be the only one if television is where people turn to for news and cultural knowledge. In a similar way, the quality of our other forms of tradition – oral and written – needs to be examined in terms of being productive means towards understanding and knowledge.

The section on the attraction of the new and the polarization of the old is directly relevant to modern cultural dynamics. Again, it shows the application of historical knowledge to reveal trends in culture, but this time the trend is immediately apparent in the modern day. The struggle between the traditional and the modern is an unfortunate but obvious outgrowth of the fast pace of communication, transportation, and change we have experienced for the past century, and will continue to experience. Any means that is set forth as a tool to provide greater understanding will inevitably have to deal with the dualism between the new and the old, and will be aligned with one or the other whether such an alignment is appropriate or not. This is because all understanding is currently processed through the lens of certain definitions that are either associated with 'traditional values' or with 'modern progress'. As long as people do not take the time to process the information they are bombarded with, this polarization will remain and continue to color the discussion. If the two sides are willing to make a legitimate debate out of the differing points of view, the polarity might actually be to the benefit of understanding. Unfortunately, neither side is willing to engage in an honest argument over the definitions, since that would risk being convinced. Neither side makes any allowance for being convinced by the other point of view – the key requirement for any constructive argument. Instead, they compete to monopolize media time and the ability to get their message out, trying to convince people not yet subsumed by the polarization. Usually, this means convincing the youth.

In the last section about perspective on the past, the scope was narrowed on a single generation. The discussion of the illusion of money and the possibility of world peace was sparked by a very simple question – why, after the horrors of the two world wars, do we resort to war even more often than we did before to solve political problems? In the fifty years after the Second World War, the United States alone fought three major wars despite the fact that the country's land was not once attacked by another country in all that time. The answer is simple – there is, thanks to the experience derived from the Second World War, the perception that war not only can solve political problem, but is in fact the most straightforward way to solve those problems. Of course, taking a look at the Korean War, the Vietnam War, and the First Persian Gulf War, the most successful of the three was the Korean War, and by all accounts it did not actually solve the problem. There is still no peace treaty to come out of that war – only a cease-fire – and North Korea is still very much hostile to both South Korea and the United States. This section, therefore, is very much an attack on war as a constructive means. Obviously, war is not self-justifying, but the very idea that it can lead to a solution at all can be shown to be a faulty generalization derived from the specific example of the Second World War and the manifest evil that Hitler represented and continues to represent.

In applying perspective, education, government, and law are examined. These three facets of community are meant to be productive means, but are often faulty and fail to perform their roles. A few faults are pointed out, mostly revolving around perspective and the internal nature of each institution. It has to be understood that our systems of education, government, and law, are each grand tools that we use to the

Conclusion

unknown end. We often think of these facets of communities as independent entities, and we do not hold them accountable when they deviate from their intended function. Broadly, education's failing is to assume its function is to prepare students for careers rather than for life. Government fails through its natural tendency to overemphasize security over the freedom of individuals, and the use of fear tactics to grab power. Law fails when it makes the same mistake for convenience, since the standards of order are far easier to reach than the interpretive standards of justice. Nevertheless, education, government, and law in the modern day are far improved than they were only a hundred years ago, and tend to be more productive. We need only to look at the civil rights movement to see how government and law can be transformative to the benefit of mutual understanding, and the reinforcement of the democratic principle.

Ultimately, knowledge is power, and if power in a democratic nation rests with the people, then the people must know. The means dealt with in this book primarily address this need for knowledge and the way a lack of knowledge can lead to the manipulation of the many by the few. Politically and economically, that manipulation has been the human condition through history. If we are to move on to the next stage of human development, then improving our condition is obviously both a means and an intermediate end. And, while the religious might emphasize faith as the main means by which humanity can develop, there is no reason to disregard knowledge. The presence of it has served us well, and the absence of it has done great harm.

Time and the Human Condition

Appendix I
Events in Space-Time

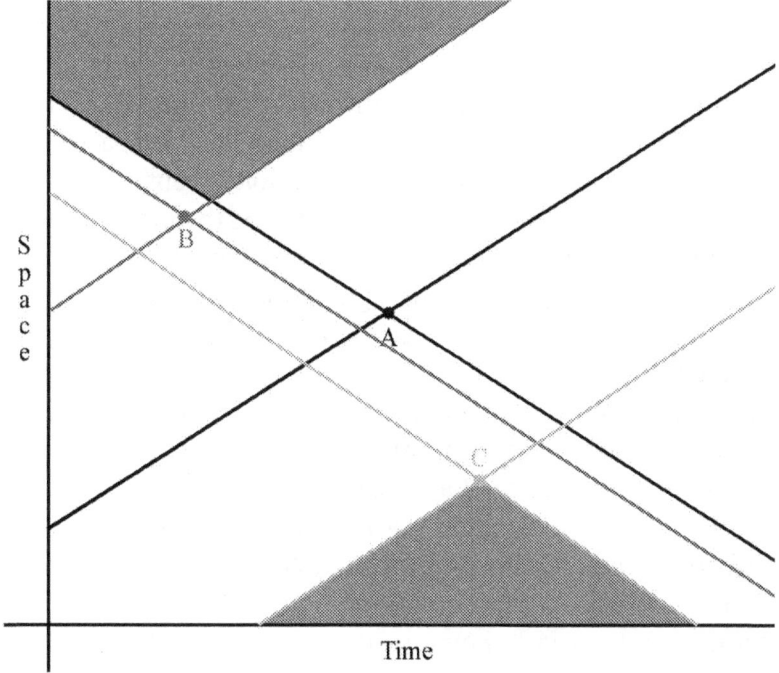

The diagram above is a two-dimensional representation of the affective past and affective future space-time cones discussed

Appendix

in the section on classical physics. In this diagram, three events are shown – A, B, and C. The diagonal lines extending to the left of each event represent the cone of the event's affective past. These cones are in negative time in relation to the event, and are limited in space by the speed of light. To the right of each event are the cones representing their affective futures. It may be difficult to imagine how this works in four dimensions when it is being shown in only two, but then trying to imagine anything in four dimensions is a trying exercise to start with.

The shaded areas on the diagram represent the areas in space-time where an event can happen, but not be caused by nor affect either A, B, or C. Notice, however, that if there was an event D in these areas, its cone would eventually overlap with that of A, B, or C, so that some event E can be in the affective past of all four, or in the affective future of all four. Eventually, everything is somehow interrelated in space-time, whether directly or through some previous event.

Event B is in the affective past of A, and therefore is within the bounds of causality, and can have had an effect on A. The point to notice about this, though, is that all of the affective future of A lies within the affective future of B. Naturally, this would have to be the case, since if B affects A, then nothing in A's affective future should be untouched by B. Also, B's entire affective past lies within the affective past of A, so that anything that might have led to B also can lead to A.

Events A and B could not have caused C, but since C's affective past overlaps with that of A and B, a single event could have been a cause of all three. Similarly, C's affective future overlaps with theirs, so that all three could be caused by a single event.

It is important to remember that, even if B was the sole cause of A, which by this diagram you can see would be almost impossible, does not mean that for an event in A's affective future, we can ignore A and ultimately say that the cause of the event was B. After all, if that were the attitude taken, then the cause of everything must necessarily be the creation of the universe, and there would be no need to discuss other events at all. At the current point in the development of our consciousness, we have to look at the smaller events and into details to try to gain knowledge and perspective. Without some concerted process, we cannot leap into comprehension of the universe, the eternal, and transcend time. For now, looking at ultimate causes helps us in only one way – to allow us to turn away from the details for a moment and get a sense of the bigger picture, to remind us to study, but not to become attached to individual experience, culture, and history, because they all involve only a tiny portion of the vast expanse of time.

When quantum mechanics is accused of violating the rules of causation, it is being accused of violating the rules behind the diagram. For instance, as discussed in terms of Bell's theorem, quantum mechanics has theorized situations that involve instantaneous influence. That would be like having an event directly under A in the diagram having an influence over A. The event is outside A's cones of causation, which are limited by the speed of light. So the influence must somehow travel past the speed of light, which is impossible under classical physics.

Even if quantum mechanics is correct, and local causation is not, the diagram of space-time causation still has conceptual value, since the limit of the speed of light is still a practical presence. In fact, using affective past and affective future to get a better grasp on history is also possible. For most of human history, communication has not traveled past the speeds managed by ships and beasts of burden, except by simple signals like beacon lights. So, though it is not valid in physics, it is perfectly logical in human affairs to narrow the cone down

Appendix

from the speed of light as the limit to the speed of communication in a given era. For instance, until the invention of the telegraph, causation in terms of human action in historical sense rarely transcended a fifty miles per hour limit. The significance of this is that today, with our better communications, more events can affect more human affairs more often. Communications has transformed history first by limiting it, then by making it unbelievably complex.

Appendix II
A Tool for Understanding History

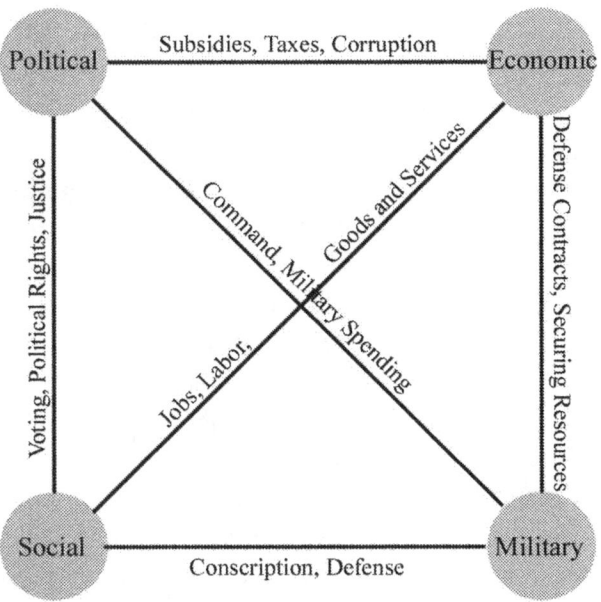

The chart above is a conceptual tool to help organize historical perspective. Using this chart, complex events can be broken

Appendix

down into four spheres – the Political, the Economic, the Military, and the Social – and their interactions. The entire chart might be called a system, which might be a city-state, a country, a kingdom, or any sort of community. Along the interaction lines I have written some of the common modern elements that might help people to understand what the interactions are. When studying history, though, a person would not be so vague as to consider 'taxes' or 'defense' along these lines, but rather more be more detailed and examine specific trends within such broad topics. Organizing those specifics can be troublesome if the only guidelines are time and geography.

The four spheres are by no means solid, and a person might replace them with spheres that make sense to himself or herself, but these four happen to also correspond to four large disciplines that history interacts with – Political Science, Economics, Sociology, and Military History. These four disciplines produce theories that help to explain certain phenomena within the spheres, and occasionally discuss one sphere's interaction with another. If a person organizes his understanding of history into these four from the start, it becomes easier to find the relevant theories to explain an event. There are other areas of study history is involved with – Archaeology, Anthropology, Linguistics, and the Arts, for instance – but these are generally tapped to draw conclusions about evidence and remains of older cultures.

While in many cases many phenomena can be fit within one sphere or another, most of the most interesting parts of history deal with either the interaction of two spheres, or the interaction between two entire systems. In the latter case, a clash of the charts, it is always intriguing to note the differences in the spheres and their interactions between the two systems, and from this comparison of the internal workings of the two systems, see where the most heated conflict might take place.

It should be noted that in all systems, there is actually a hierarchy between the four spheres, so that one dominates above the rest and can often determine how the others relate to each other. In the United States today, it is clear that the economic realm is dominant. During the medieval era, the political realm was dominant in most countries because the nobility commanded the economy, supplied military might, and built society around themselves. It might be argued that society was dominant in ancient Athens, though that would be a subject of deep debate. In warrior societies like that of Japan during the period of Warring States, around 1485 to 1603, the military sphere is clearly superior to the rest.

The position of spirituality and culture in the chart is vital to note. Culture is solely a matter of the social realm, because it exercises its greatest power through social norms, and mediates the interactions between individuals. The degree to which culture emanating from the social sphere affects the other spheres indicates the relative strength of society. If the other spheres have a massive impact on culture, that indicates a relative weakness in the social sphere. In the United States, we have what is called a consumer culture. As the name implies, there is a clear dominance of economics over society, and it is difficult for us to imagine a time when elements of culture did not need to be purchased.

Spirituality is more dynamic than culture because, to an absolute degree, it is meant to be above all of history. Of course, spirituality as it has been practiced has often been intertwined with the spheres. Sometimes various beliefs systems have tried to control a few or all of the spheres, and at other times the spheres have had their impact on spirituality. Religion, in particular, can actually come to dominate all of the spheres. In Medieval Europe, the Pope held immense power in the political realm – to the point that one pontiff outright claimed supremacy over all the kings of Europe in

Appendix

both the temporal sense as well as the spiritual. Contributing to this political power was derived from the fact the Catholic Church was the largest single landholder in Europe – controlling not only the Papal States, but also church lands in every country – so that it was also the single most important economic power as well. While its military power was only moderate, the Church could call on all the kings of Europe to launch a crusade. The Church's impact on society, of course, varied from locality to locality, but if the Church opposed a cultural element, it would have been difficult for that element to stand. In the modern era, of course, the same kind of religious control over every sphere can be seen in the Muslim world. It is clear, though, that when spirituality becomes more involved with the matters of the four spheres, particularly when it gets entangled with culture, that involvement takes time away from the broadening of spiritual understanding.

In the contemporary United States, religion is expressly prohibited from dominating the political realm, and never had real economic power, though in both cases the more powerful churches still try and gain influence. While religion has some influence in the military, churches do not actually have military power as they had in the medieval age. Instead of rising above the four spheres of the historical system, however, most forms of spirituality in the United States, Christian or otherwise, get focused into the social realm, and are entangled with culture. Part of the reason for this is a legacy from the way Western Europe removed the influence of the Catholic Church from temporal institutions. Because of its current confinement, spirituality is often mistaken for a facet of culture, or more tightly related to culture than it should be.

These dynamics can all be seen clearly once the events and interactions of history are sorted out. Using different spheres, a different view of history would result, but the conclusions derived from such a variation should only deepen a person's understanding of history. The diagram presented above is meant as a starting point.

Appendix

Inspirational and Spiritual Titles from Alight Publications

Dew-Drops of the Soul
Yogiraj Gurunath Siddhanath

Earth Peace through Self Peace
Yogiraj Gurunath Siddhanath

Wings to Freedom
Yogiraj Gurunath Siddhanath

Chakra selfHealing by the Power of Om
Rudra Shivananda

Surya Yoga
Rudra Shivananda

Breathe like your Life Depends on It
Rudra Shivananda

Yoga of Purification and Transformation
Rudra Shivananda

**For information on our titles or to order them, visit:
htttp://www.Alightbooks.com**

www.ingramcontent.com/pod-product-compliance
Lightning Source LLC
LaVergne TN
LVHW011347080426
835511LV00005B/168